WOODWORKING

Favorite Projects and Techniques

Edited by Al Gutierrez

Meredith® Press
New York

Meredith® Press is an imprint of Meredith® Books:

President, Book Group: Joseph J. Ward
Vice President, Editorial Director: Elizabeth P. Rice

Executive Editor: Connie Schrader
Art Director: Ernest Shelton
Project Manager: Marsha Jahns
Production Manager: Bill Rose

Cover Photo: Jonathan Press

Cover Photo: California Redwood Association

For Jonathan Press and Skil Corporation:

Produced by Jonathan Press, Cannon Falls, MN
Producer/Executive Director: Al Gutierrez
Senior Editor: Dianne Talmage
Copy Editor: Cheryl Clark
Technical Consultant: Gary Branson
Editorial Assistant: Sandra Hadler
Illustrator: Geri Klug
Illustrator: Eugene Marino III
Draftsman: Jimmilee Miller
Woodworking Technician: Jeremy Irrthum
Woodworking Technician: Pat Manion
Woodworking Technician: Wesley Clark
Photo Stylist/Artist: Sharon Doucette

Brief quotations may be used in critical articles and reviews. For any other reproduction of the book, however, including electronic, mechanical, photocopying, recording or other means, written permission must be obtained from the publisher.

The designs in this book are the copyrighted property of the craftsmen and craftswomen who built them. Readers are encouraged to produce these projects for their personal use or for gifts. However, reproduction for sale or profit is forbidden by law.

The projects presented in this book have come from a variety of sources. The plans and instructions have been developed by many different writers. We have tried to select those projects that will assure accuracy and safety. Due to differing conditions, tools, and individual technical skills, Meredith® Press assumes no responsibility for any injuries suffered, damages or losses incurred during, or as a result of, the construction of these projects.

Before starting on any project, study the plans carefully; read and observe all the safety precautions provided by any tool or equipment manufacturer and follow all accepted safety procedures during construction.

ISBN: 0-696-11136-5

10 9 8 7 6 5 4 3 2 1

TABLE OF CONTENTS

INDOOR PROJECTS

OUTDOOR PROJECTS

SPECIAL TOOL SECTION: SABER SAWS

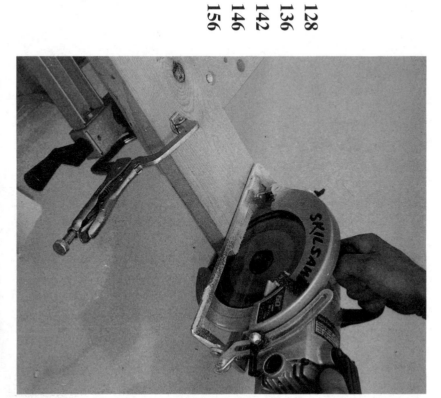

INDOOR PROJECTS

Dry Sink

Many antique collectors and pottery enthusiasts include a dry sink on their wish lists. This traditional dry sink will blend in with most decors and when built with No. 2 pine, can be squeezed into most budgets.

Our dry sink features two wide doors to access roomy storage space for dishes, cups and saucers — even glassware. The dry sink itself is deep and sturdy, making it a great place for displaying plants, knick-knacks or the traditional bowl and pitcher. The three top drawers are ideal for storing napkins, napkin holders, salt and pepper shakers and other dining accessories.

SKILL LEVEL. Woodworkers with moderate to advanced woodworking skills will find the dry sink a challenging project. The greatest complexity is forming the raised door panels in the two doors.

TIPS. No. 2 pine is quite suitable for this project. The wood's knots add character to the unit and are in keeping with the project's traditional design. If you do not care for the simplicity of pine, oak is a very good alternative. Its only drawback is that it is much more expensive than No. 2 pine.

Old-fashioned detailing is combined with modern-day practicality to make this classic dry sink a budget-stretching beauty.

CONSTRUCTION. The sides (A) and the shelves (B) must be formed from several pieces of narrower material, edge-glued together. Carefully select the workpieces and joint them for edge-gluing. Check the tightness of the joints prior to gluing to ensure that there are no gaps and that you do not have to tighten the clamps excessively in order to close the joint. Then use a good carpenter's glue (yellow glue) to edge-glue these components. Allow the glue to cure for 24 hours, and then use a paint scraper to remove any glue that has oozed from the joint.

Cut the sides and the shelves to their overall widths and lengths. Then make the cutouts in the side workpieces by stacking them on top of one another and using a circular saw guided with a straight-edge. You will not be able to finish the inside cuts with a circular saw, so use a saber saw or a handsaw instead.

Set up a dado blade in your table saw to cut a ¾ in. wide by ⅜ in. deep cut. Then make the dado and rabbet cuts in each of the two side pieces.

Depending on the size of your table saw, you may have to make a special auxiliary holding table to stabilize the side workpiece while dadoing. If you are totally unfamiliar with this technique or do not have

Dry Sink

a table saw, make the rabbets and dadoes using a router equipped with a ¾ in. wide rabbeting bit and guided with a straightedge.

Next, cut out the top (C), top shelf (D), top rail (F), stiles (G, I) and bottom rail (H). Rip them slightly wider and finish them on your jointer.

Now, cut dadoes into the top (C) and the top shelf (D) to accommodate the two dividers (M).

Clean out all of the dado cuts with a sharp wood chisel, making sure that all of the project parts fit snugly together without any gaps.

Dry-assemble the top and the shelf to the two sides and custom measure the two dividers (M). Cut the dividers on your table saw.

Readjust your saw's dado blade to cut a ¼ in. wide by ⅜ in. deep rabbet along the two sides and the top.

Cut the back (E) to size using a circular saw

equipped with a plywood cutting blade.

Lay out the bottom rail design. Equip your saber saw with a fine-tooth blade, such as a plywood cutting blade, and make your cut. Then smooth the contour with a drum sander installed in a portable drill.

ASSEMBLY OF MAIN UNIT. The next phase calls for assembling the main unit with carpenter's glue and 4d finishing nails. Begin by attaching the dividers (M) to the top (C) and the shelf (D) and, in turn, attaching this assembly along with the remaining shelves (B) to the two sides. Square the assembly, and then attach the back (E) using brads and carpenter's glue. Make sure that the unit is square. Allow the glue to dry overnight.

Double-check the fit of the stiles (G, I) and the rails (F, H) to ensure that they do not protrude beyond the sides of the cabinet. Note that in some carcass

TONGUE AND GROOVING THE DOORS

Figure 1.

Groove the four door stiles (J) with a dado blade installed in the table saw. Keep the workpiece firmly against the fence, making sure the groove is directly in the middle.

Figure 2.

After grooving the four door rails (K), cut the tongues. Cut one edge, then flip the workpiece 180 degrees and cut the other edge.

constructions, a protrusion of 1/8 in. beyond the surface is acceptable.

Secure the stiles and the rails to one another before attaching them to the, dry sink with glue and wood dowels. Use two dowels at each joint. You can also substitute plate joint biscuits for dowels. Instead of clamping the stiles and rails together at this point, attach them to the dry sink with glue and finishing nails. Use clamps only where necessary to ensure a tight joint.

DRAWERS. Measure the dry sink's drawer cavities and construct the drawers, allowing a 1/8 in. gap on both the left and right drawer sides as well as the top. Cut out the drawer fronts/backs (N) and the drawer sides (O) on your table saw. Now, cut rabbets into the drawer fronts/backs with a dado blade installed on your table saw. When you are finished,

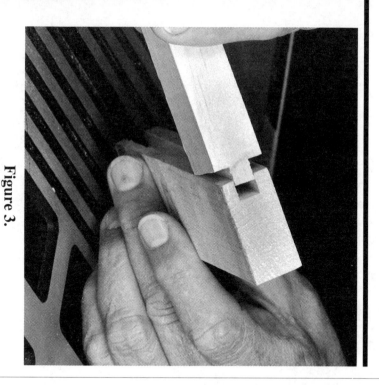

Figure 3.
The door rails (K) should fit firmly into the door stiles (J).

If you do not have a table saw to cut the dadoes and rabbets into the sides (A), use a router. Install a straight bit and use a clamped straightedge to guide the router. Maintain a firm grip on the router and make light passes until the router bit achieves the final depth.

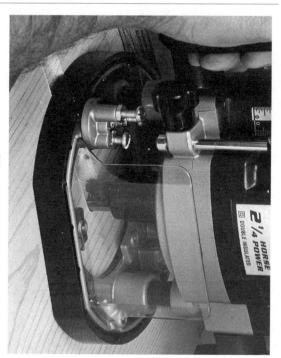

Figure 4.

readjust the dado blade to cut a 1/4 in. wide by 1/4 in. deep groove, and then groove all of the drawer parts. These grooves will accommodate the drawer bottoms (P).

Next, cut all of the plywood drawer bottoms. Assemble the drawers with the drawer bottoms using carpenter's glue and 1 in. brads. Do not glue or nail the plywood bottoms. Make sure that each set of drawers is square.

Locate the positions for the porcelain knobs. Drill holes for the knobs into the drawer fronts, using a backup board to avoid splintering the wood.

DOORS. Each of the two doors feature a raised panel that can be formed on your table saw. Begin by cutting out the door stiles (J) along with the door rails (K). Notice that the drawer rails have tongues on the

3/4" X 3/8" Deep rabbet for top.

3/4" X 3/8" Deep dado

3/4"

3/4"

3/4"

6"

9"

10"

3 1/2"

2"

17"

16 3/4"

14 3/4"

2"

1 1/2" Hinges

1 1/2"

2"

3 1/2"

A

G

J

K

L

K

J

H

F

B

M

D

N

M

Use dowels and glue to attach middle stile to top and bottom rail.

3/4" X 3/8" Dado for dividers

29 1/4"

30"

9"

3/4"

9"

3/4"

N

O

N

N

O

C

12"

24"

36"

B

A

E

B

G

J

K

L

K

J

G

2" (TYP.)

1"

1"

1 1/4"

14"

2"

3/4" X 3/8" Deep dado as required for shelves.

3/8"X 1/4"Deep rabbet in sides and top for back.

2"

6 1/4"

10 1/4"

2"

See door detail for floating panel and mortise and tenon dimensions.

H

1/4"X 1/4" groove for bottom (all around)

3"

5 3/4"

8 3/4"

O

N

N

O

P

1/2"X 1/4"Deep rabbet for sides.

12

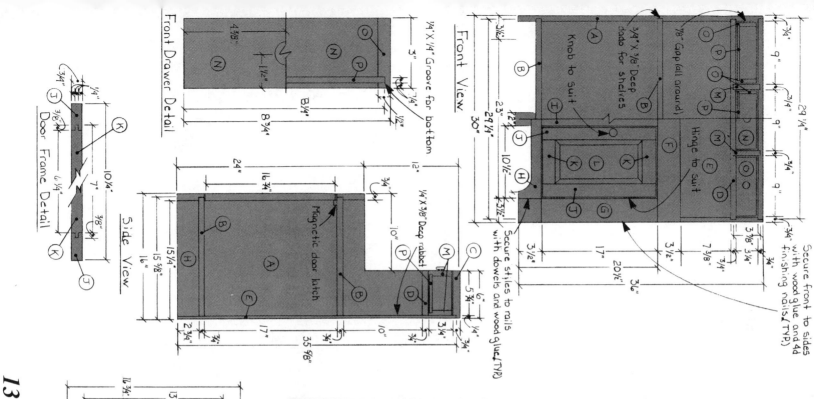

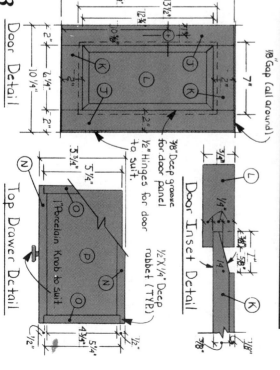

Front View

Side View

Front Drawer Detail

Door Frame Detail

Door Detail

Door Inset Detail

Top Drawer Detail

13

Front View labels and notes:
- 3/4" x 3/8" dado for shelves
- 1/8" Gap (all around)
- Knob to suit
- Hinge to suit
- Secure front to sides with wood glue and 4d finishing nails (TYP)
- Secure stiles to rails with dowels and wood glue (TYP)

Side View notes:
- Magnetic door latch
- 1/4" x 3/8" Deep rabbet

Front Drawer Detail:
- 1/4" X 1/4" Groove for bottom

Door Detail:
- 1/8" Gap (all around)

Door Inset Detail:
- 3/8" Deep groove for door panel
- 1/2"X 1/4" Deep rabbet (TYP)
- 1/2" Hinges for door to suit

Top Drawer Detail:
- Porcelain Knob to suit

Cutting List

A	Side	3/4 x 15 1/4 x 36		2
B	Shelf	3/4 x 15 3/8 x 29 1/4		2
C	Top	3/4 x 6 x 29 1/4		1
D	Top shelf	3/4 x 5 3/4 x 29 1/4		1
E	Back	1/4 x 29 1/4 x 35 5/8	plywood	1
F	Top rail	3/4 x 3 1/2 x 30		1
G	Stile	3/4 x 3 1/2 x 20 1/2		1
H	Bottom rail	3/4 x 3 1/2 x 23		1
I	Middle stile	3/4 x 2 x 17		1
J	Door stile	3/4 x 2 x 16 3/4		4
K	Door rail	3/4 x 2 x 7		4
L	Door panel	1/2 x 7 x 13 1/2		2
M	Divider	3/4 x 4 x 5 3/4		2
N	Drawer front/back	1/2 x 3 x 8 3/4		6
O	Drawer sides	1/2 x 3 x 5 1/4		6
P	Drawer bottom	1/4 x 4 3/4 x 8 1/4	plywood	3

Note: All material is pine unless otherwise indicated. All dimensions are in inches.

Dry Sink

ends that must be cut out. Then cut the two door panels (L) to width and length.

Set up your table saw to cut a ¼ in. wide by ⅜ in. deep groove, and then groove all of the door stiles (J). Note that the groove must be precisely in the center of the workpiece. We suggest making test cuts in scrap material before working on the final workpieces.

Now, groove the door rails (K). Readjust the table saw's fence to cut the pins into the door rails. Dry-assemble each of the two doors to make sure that the joints are snug. If they are too tight, shave some of the wood off the pins in the rails (K) with a sharp wood chisel.

Next, set up your table saw to cut the door panels (L). The saw blade must be tilted to an angle of 14 degrees and set to the appropriate cutting height. If

everything is set up correctly, the blade will break through the surface of the panel as it cuts to the desired angle. Again, you must make repetitive test cuts to ensure that everything fits properly. After you have made the test cut along the edge of scrap material, fit the test workpiece into the groove of one of the door rails to ensure that it fits properly. When everything is exact, cut all four sides of each door panel on your table saw.

Dry-assemble each door along with the raised panels to make sure that everything fits properly. If not, you may have to do some sanding or recutting on your table saw.

Use a palm sander to remove the saw marks from the bevels cut in the raised panels now, because it is impossible to do a good job once the panels are

FORMING DOOR PANELS

Figure 5.
Tilt the saw blade on your table saw to 14 degrees and set the blade to the proper cutting height to cut the door panels (L). Rip one edge.

Figure 6.
Complete the door panel (L) cuts by turning the workpiece 90 degrees and cutting the other edge, continuing until all four edges are cut. Keep the workpiece firmly against the fence to avoid gouging the wood.

assembled. Finish sand all of the other door parts with your pad sander, being careful not to round over any edges.

Assemble each set of doors with carpenter's glue. Use glue only on the joints where the rails join the stiles. Do not glue the raised panels. The panels will expand and contract within the door frames, and if they are glued there is a strong likelihood that they will split.

Test-fit the doors to ensure that they fit properly. If they don't fit, trim with light passes on a jointer. Then mortise an area for the 1½ in. pin hinges.

FINISHING TOUCHES. Finish sand all of the project parts. A palm sander is ideal for obtaining a smooth finish in many of the project's nooks and crannies.

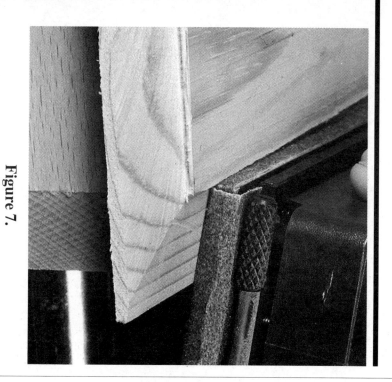

Figure 7.
Sand the door panel's beveled edge with a palm sander. Make long strokes to ensure an evenly sanded surface.

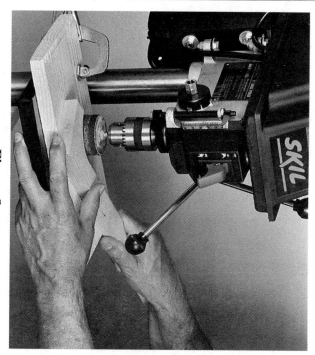

Figure 8.
After cutting out the design for the bottom rail (H), sand the contour with a drum sander installed in your drill press. Move the wood into the drum's cutting surface.

Carefully remove all of the fine dust particles with a damp (but not wet), clean cloth.

Apply a suitable wood stain for the project, according to the manufacturer's application instructions. Most instructions require that you remove heavy stain residue with a clean, lint-free cloth while wiping in the grain's direction.

Apply a good coat of clear sealer to the project with a spray gun. When the sealer has dried, follow this up with a very fine sanding.

Now, apply a satin finish and allow it to dry. Follow this up with another light sanding and a final finish application.

Hinge the two doors and install all of the door and drawer knobs. Install one magnetic latch for each of the two doors. These, of course, hold the doors in place but also prevent the doors from being pushed inside the cabinet.

❖

16

Antique Display Table

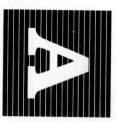

A display table can brighten up just about any spot in your home. Use it to display your favorite items and at the same time add a focal point to any room. This display table offers lots of eye-catching features yet takes up little space. Its contours and interesting lines make it as attention-getting as the items displayed on it!

SKILL LEVEL. The antique display table is well suited for intermediate to advanced woodworkers.

TIPS. A pantograph is the ideal aid for enlarging the leg pattern.

CONSTRUCTION.

Begin by laying out the top (A) and the shelf (B) on solid oak lumber, using a flexible curve. Flexible curves can be purchased at art or drafting supply stores.

Cut out the design on a band saw and then smooth the edges with a stationary disk sander or an abrasive sander.

Carefully transfer the design for the legs (C) onto solid, knot-free oak, using a pantograph or graph paper. Once you are satisfied with the transfer design, cut out the leg pattern with your band saw. Use a narrow blade.

Sand the leg contours with a stationary abrasive belt sander. Then transfer the finished leg pattern onto

Here's the perfect enhancement for a long hallway or an empty wall.

(A), the shelf (B) and the decorative edge (D).

Notice that the leg has a special design cut into part of its contour. Refer to the illustration. Set up your router table and carefully rout each of the three legs.

ASSEMBLY. Secure the decorative edge (D) to the top (A) with carpenter's glue and No. 8 by 1¼ in.

the other two leg workpieces. Process the remaining legs the same way you did the first leg.

Each of the three leg brackets (E) requires a wide and deep groove. Instead of cutting each of the brackets to length, lay them out on longer material and cut the grooves into this longer material. Now, cut the grooves into this longer material. Now, cut the radiused corners using your band saw, and then use your table saw to crosscut each bracket to its final length.

The 1 in. thick decorative edge (D) follows the same contours as the top (A), except that the decorative edge is set ¾ in. in from the top's edge. Lay out the contour for the decorative edge, making the edge 1½ in. wide. This decorative edge will conceal the brackets once they are installed underneath the tabletop. Cut the decorative edge's contour on your band saw and then sand the edge smooth with an abrasive sander.

Install router bits in your router table to produce the edges in the top workpiece

17

Figure 1.

Cut out the leg pattern with a band saw equipped with a 1/4 in. or narrower blade.

18

flathead wood screws. Countersink all of the screw heads.

Attach one bracket to each leg with carpenter's glue and one No. 8 by 1¼ in. flathead wood screw. Make sure that you predrill these holes and countersink the screw heads.

Dry-assemble the project, positioning each leg so it approximates our finished project. Mark the leg positions underneath the top (A) as well as underneath the shelf (B). You must use a square to ensure that each leg is perfectly perpendicular to the floor as well as to the top and the shelf.

This project is courtesy of Pat and Ann Manion. How-to photographs are courtesy of Skil Corporation.

Cutting List

A	Top	¾ x 10⅞ x 28	1
B	Shelf	¾ x 6⅞ x 22	1
C	Leg	1 x 4½ x 28	3
D	Decorative edge	1 x 10⅛ x 26½	1
E	Leg bracket	1½ x 1¾ x 4	3

Note: All material is oak unless otherwise indicated. All dimensions are in inches.

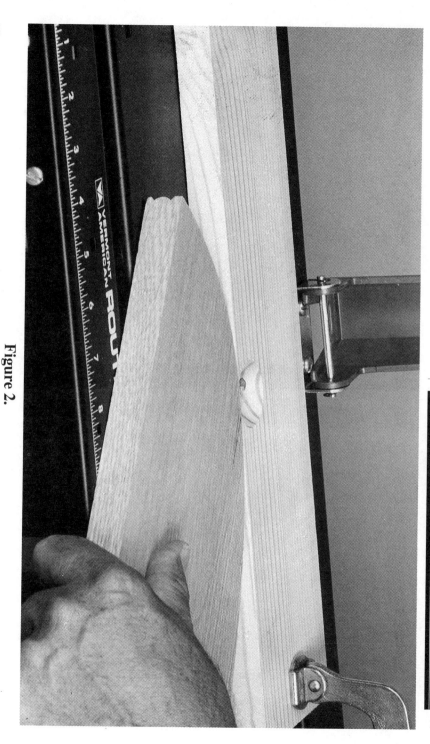

Figure 2.

Use a router table to mill the beaded edge into the shelf (B). The guard is lifted for clarity.

Antique Display Table

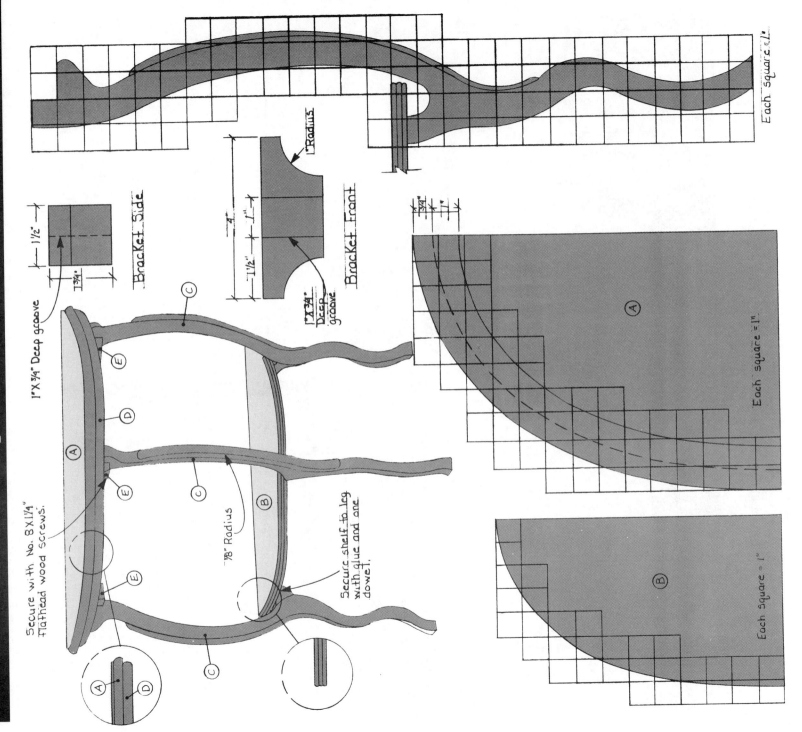

Each square = 1"

1" X ¾" Deep groove

Secure with No. 8X1¼"
Flathead wood screws.

Bracket Side

1½"

¾"

1" Radius

Bracket Front

4"

1"

1½"

1"

"1X¾"
Deep
groove

⅞" Radius

Secure shelf to leg
with glue and one
dowel.

Each square = 1".

Each square = 1"

20

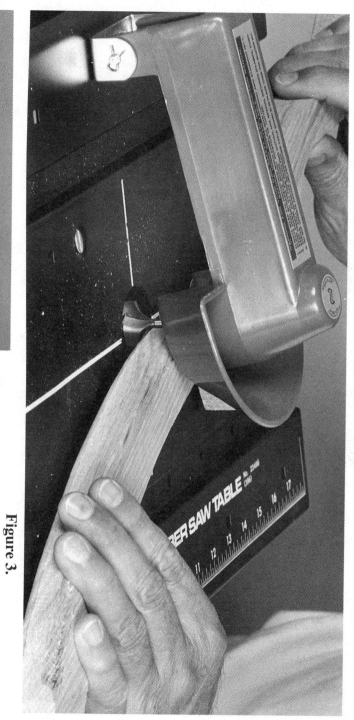

Figure 3.
Carefully rout the design into part of the leg contour, using a router bit installed on your router table.

Disassemble the unit and drill matching dowel holes to connect the lower part of the legs to the shelf (B).

Now, reassemble the project by installing the shelf onto the doweled legs with carpenter's glue. Also, apply glue to the top of the brackets and mount them underneath the top (A) with No. 8 by 1¼ in. flathead wood screws. Drive two screws into each bracket, countersinking the screw heads. Again, check to make sure that the entire unit is square.

FINISHING. Allow the glue to dry for at least 24 hours. Then finish sand the entire project and use a damp, but not wet, clean cloth to remove any fine dust particles. Apply the stain of your choice, followed by a coat of sanding sealer. After the sanding sealer has dried, give the project a light sanding to remove any dust residue. Now, apply one or more coats of a satin polyurethane finish to complete your project.

Figure 4.
An abrasive sander is an ideal tool for sanding the many contoured areas of the project parts.

21

❖

Contemporary Coffee Table

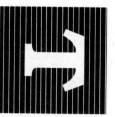

his versatile piece of furniture serves a dual purpose. It's a handsome coffee table for contemporary settings, and it's a handy storage center. The three large drawers help hide the endless accumulation of papers that seems to always clutter any available surface. There's room for all of your remotes, newspapers and TV guides. On the outside, special finishing touches such as inset brass drawer pulls allow you to blend the table with your decor. The table is also cost effective to build, requiring only 1½ sheets of APA structural wood panels.

SKILL LEVEL. This is a good project for both beginning and intermediate-level woodworkers. If cutting dadoes and rabbets are difficult for you, substitute butt joints to make the job easier.

TIPS. We recommend using a circular saw and a table saw to cut the project parts. Equip both tools with a plywood cutting blade or with a hollow ground

This coffee table with built-in storage space will enhance the formal decor of a living room or the casual atmosphere of a family room.

planer blade. This will minimize wood splintering and produce smoother cuts.

To obtain an attractive, professional-looking finish, we suggest using a spray gun to apply the paint. An air-driven or airless type will work best. Also, use an APA A-B interior plywood for a smooth finish and to cut down on sanding time.

CONSTRUCTION. Carefully lay out all of your project parts with the aid of a straightedge and a carpenter's square. It is best to cut out the larger parts with a circular saw. A 4x8 sheet of plywood is difficult to handle on a table saw.

Use your circular saw in combination with a straightedge to make crosscuts on long workpieces such as the top (A). It is also a good idea to cut with the good side down to minimize the splintering that can show on a final project.

Install a dado blade in your table saw to cut the ³⁄₄ in. wide by ¹⁄₄ in. deep dadoes and rabbets required for the top and bottom workpieces (A). Similarly, cut the rabbets for the base

table saw to cut the project parts and rabbets required for the pieces (A). Similarly, cut the fronts and backs (D).

Contemporary Coffee Table

Figure 1.

Use a circular saw guided with a straightedge to cut the 4x8 sheet of plywood into smaller workpieces to prepare them for cutting on a table saw. Cutting a 4x8 sheet on a table saw can be dangerous.

Next, readjust the height of the dado blade to ½ in. deep to cut the rabbets in the drawer fronts and backs (G). You will have to carefully position the drawer fronts and backs on the table saw to obtain the proper width for the rabbet.

Readjust the table saw's dado blade to cut a ½ in. wide by ¼ in. deep groove. Then groove all of the drawer fronts and backs and the drawer sides (H) to hold the drawer bottoms (I).

Install the drawer pulls at this time. If they are similar to the drawer pulls that we included on our project, you will have to mortise an area to accommodate the back of the handle. If you have to mortise the area, use a chisel and/or a router equipped with a straight bit to form the mortise.

ASSEMBLY. Use a good carpenter's glue and 4d finishing nails to assemble the project.

Begin assembling the project by securing the top to the sides (B) and the dividers (C) with glue and finishing nails. Then attach the bottom. Make sure the assembly is square, and allow the glue to cure for 24 hours before moving the project.

This project is courtesy of the American Plywood Association, P.O. Box 11700, Tacoma, WA 98411. How-to photographs are courtesy of Skil Corporation.

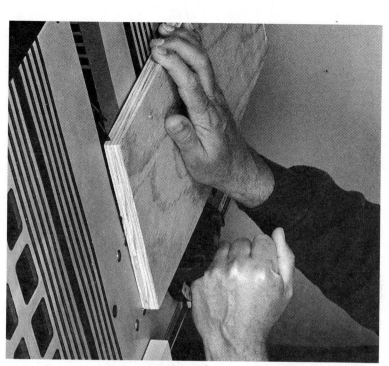

Figure 2.

To make repetitive rabbet cuts for the drawer front/back workpieces, clamp a starting block at the appropriate distance, as shown. Then move the drawer snug to the starting block while holding the workpiece firmly to the miter gauge. Next, move the workpiece into the dado blade.

Next, secure the base fronts and backs (D) to the base sides (E). Square the assembly by adding the three base supports (F).

Install the base to the coffee table with 3d finishing nails. Drive the nails from underneath the base, nailing through the base supports and up into the bottom (A). Remember to use glue as well.

Assemble all three drawers by attaching the drawer fronts and backs (G) to the drawer sides (H). Install the drawer bottoms (I) at this time. There is no need to glue the drawer bottoms because they will float within the dadoes created in the drawer fronts,

backs and sides. Carefully make sure that each drawer unit is square, and allow the glue to cure for 24 hours.

SAFETY FIRST. Before spray painting, select an appropriate place in which to paint, such as a well-ventilated garage. Make sure to cover the floor as well as any items that could get a coat of overspray. Also, wear a dust mask and eye protection. Be sure to read the manufacturer's instructions for thinning and applying these solvents.

FINISHING. Remove the drawer pulls. Sink all nailheads with a punch, then fill in all project blemishes with a strong nontoxic wood filler. Finish sand all of the project parts, making sure to slightly dull all the showing edges with a sanding block or a palm sander.

Inspect the project to ensure that the inside cavity of the coffee table does not have any excess glue that may prevent the drawers from sliding properly.

Cutting List

A	Top/bottom	3/4 x 23¹⁵/₁₆ x 47	2
B	Side	3/4 x 8 x 23¹⁵/₁₆	2
C	Divider	3/4 x 8½ x 23¹⁵/₁₆	2
D	Base front/ back	3/4 x 3¾ x 44	2
E	Base side	3/4 x 3¾ x 19	2
F	Base support	3/4 x 2½ x 18½	3
G	Drawer front/ back	3/4 x 7⅞ x 14⅞	6
H	Drawer side	½ x 7⅞ x 23⅜	6
I	Drawer bottom	½ x 14⅞ x 21⅞	3

Note: All material is plywood unless otherwise indicated. All dimensions are in inches.

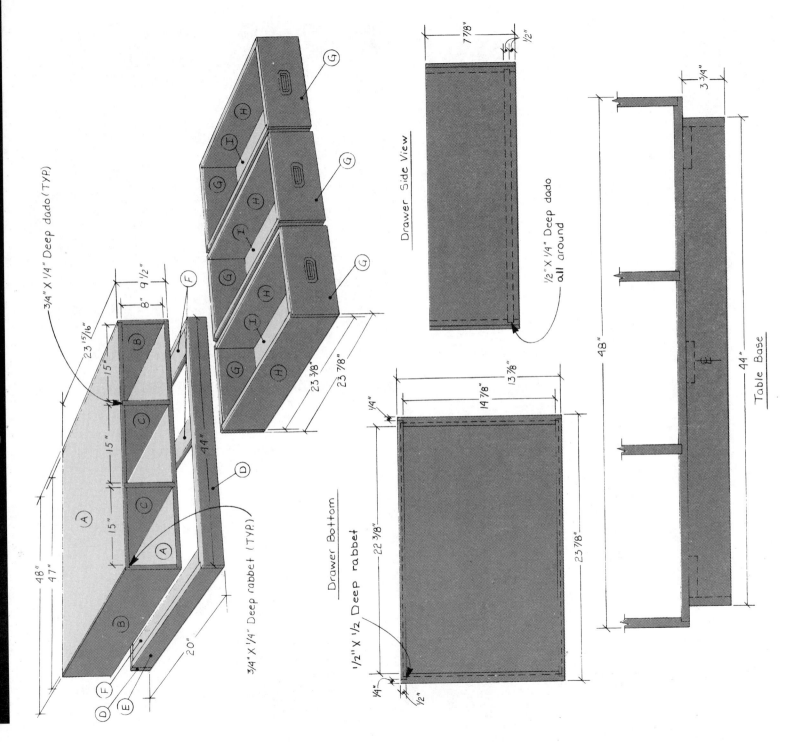

3/4" X 1/4" Deep dado (TYP.)

23 15/16"

8"

9 1/2"

15"

15"

15"

15"

48"

47"

20"

3/4" X 1/4" Deep rabbet (TYP.)

(A)

(B)

(C)

(C)

(A)

(B)

(D)

(E)

(F)

(F)

(D)

23 3/8"

23 7/8"

(G)

(G)

(G)

(H)

(I)

(G)

(H)

(I)

(G)

(H)

(I)

Drawer Side View

7 7/8"

1/2"

1/2" X 1/4" Deep dado all around

Drawer Bottom

1/4"

14 7/8"

13 7/8"

22 3/8"

23 7/8"

1/2" X 1/2 Deep rabbet

1/4"

1/2"

48"

3 3/4"

44"

Table Base

26

Figure 3.

Smooth the dadoes with a sharp wood chisel. You must securely clamp the workpiece to the workbench to avoid accidents. If you do not clean the dado cut, you will have a gap and the joint will not be as strong.

Use a shop vac to carefully clean all surfaces of the project. Then use a damp (not wet), clean cloth to remove fine sawdust.

Spray paint an oil-base sealer onto all of the surfaces of the project, including the insides of the drawers. Allow the sealer to dry thoroughly and then give it a light sanding.

Follow this up with a coat of your favorite paint. When the project is dry, give it a light sanding and then apply the final coat.

Apply wax to the inside bottom of the coffee table, where the drawers slide. Ask the retailer who sold you the paint to recommend an appropriate wax. Apply one or two coats of wax. This will allow the drawers to slide more easily and will reduce friction that could mar the project's paint.

❖ ──────────────

27

Figure 4.

Use a wood chisel to mortise the area for recessed drawer pulls, if necessary. Some hardware may not require mortises. Exercise caution, and clamp the drawer fronts/backs to the bench for safety. Carefully lay out the area to be mortised, and use a carving gouge and a regular wood chisel to process this area.

Pine Knife Box

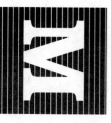 ealtime is a little easier when you already have the silverware on the table! Although this pine box was intended to hold silverware, it has many other uses. You can use it to house cloth napkins, or heap it with fresh fruit, colorful gourds or silk flowers for an attractive display piece. We have added tole painting to our rendition of the pine knife box to create a festive look. You can duplicate the pattern we have included, but feel free to use your imagination. This project offers lots of opportunities for personalization.

SKILL LEVEL. The knife box is quite suitable for the intermediate-level woodworker.

TIPS. This project requires cutting precise compound angles. If you are not confident in your cutting skills, cut the four sides (A, B) wider and cut only the handle (C) and the bottom (D) to fit.

CONSTRUCTION. Cut the sides (A, B) to their overall widths, but cut them about ½ in. longer. Then set up your table saw to cut the compound angle called for in the illustration. Set the miter gauge at the designated angle, then make test cuts on several scrap workpieces to ensure that everything fits properly. Now, make your cuts in the actual workpieces.

Next, using your table saw, bevel both long edges of each of the four sides. Again, test cut on scrap workpieces to guarantee accuracy. When you are satisfied, cut the actual workpieces.

Cut the bottom (D) to size and rout over the top edges. Dry-assemble the sides onto the bottom to make sure there are no gaps. If there are gaps, you will have to recut the edges' bevels.

When the workpieces are perfect, attach the sides to one another with glue and No. 8 by 1½ in. flathead wood screws. Counterbore all screw heads and cut plugs to fill in the recesses.

Secure the bottom to the assembled sides with glue and wood screws. This time, countersink the fastener heads.

Measure the inside cavity of the box before forming the handle (C). Using your table saw, cut the angled ends of the handle. Next, draw the pattern for the contour onto the workpiece and cut to shape with a band saw.

Now, lay out the handhold. Drill two starter holes at each end of the handhold, using a backer board to prevent wood splintering. Then cut out the section in between with a saber saw equipped with a plywood cutting blade.

Equip your router table with a ⅜ in. rounding over bit and rout the handle as well as the handhold. Install the handle using wood screws and glue. Again, counterbore the screw heads and plug the recesses.

Add a touch of country to your dining room table with this sturdy pine box.

Pine Knife Box

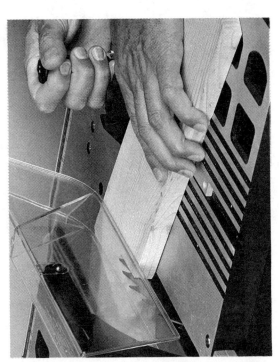

Figure 2.

Cut the compound angles required for each of the sides (A, B) on your table saw. You will need to use your miter gauge.

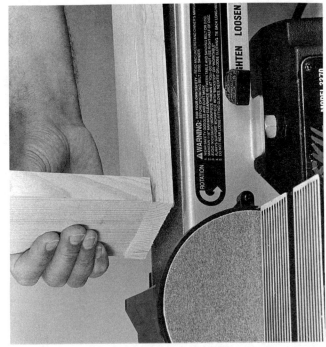

Figure 4.

Sand the plugs flush with a stationary sander as shown.

Figure 1.

Rip the bevels into the long edges of the sides (A, B) on the table saw.

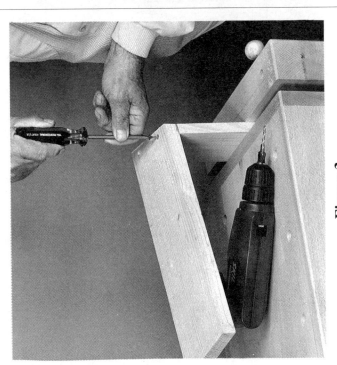

Figure 3.

Secure the sides (A, B) to one another with glue and flathead wood screws. Counterbore each fastener hole.

Tole Painting the Knife Box

Sharon Doucette, a craftsperson and artist, came up with this knife box design, which she painted using a technique that is a cross between tole painting and Bavarian art.

Before you begin painting the project, you must first apply at least one light coat of varnish. This will prevent the paint from bleeding into the wood. If you prefer to stain the project, stain also will provide an adequate base for painting.

Trace the design pattern from the enlarged photo that we have included in this story and then further enlarge it on a copy machine until it is the size you want. Follow this up by tracing the design onto the wood, using graphite paper placed between the design pattern and the wood. After you have outlined the design, you are ready to paint.

Apply the tole paint with a small paintbrush. It is best to apply one color at a time. The paints and brushes can be purchased at most craft shops.

Unfortunately, learning the fine art of tole painting is not something that we can easily cover here. It is best to take a class in tole painting, or you can simply experiment.

Figure 5.
Here Sharon is drawing her original design on a full-size template of the knife box front.

Figure 6.
Now she transfers the pattern onto the actual workpiece with the aid of graphite paper.

Figure 7.
Finally, Sharon applies one color at a time to the design pattern.

31

How-to photographs are courtesy of Skil Corporation.

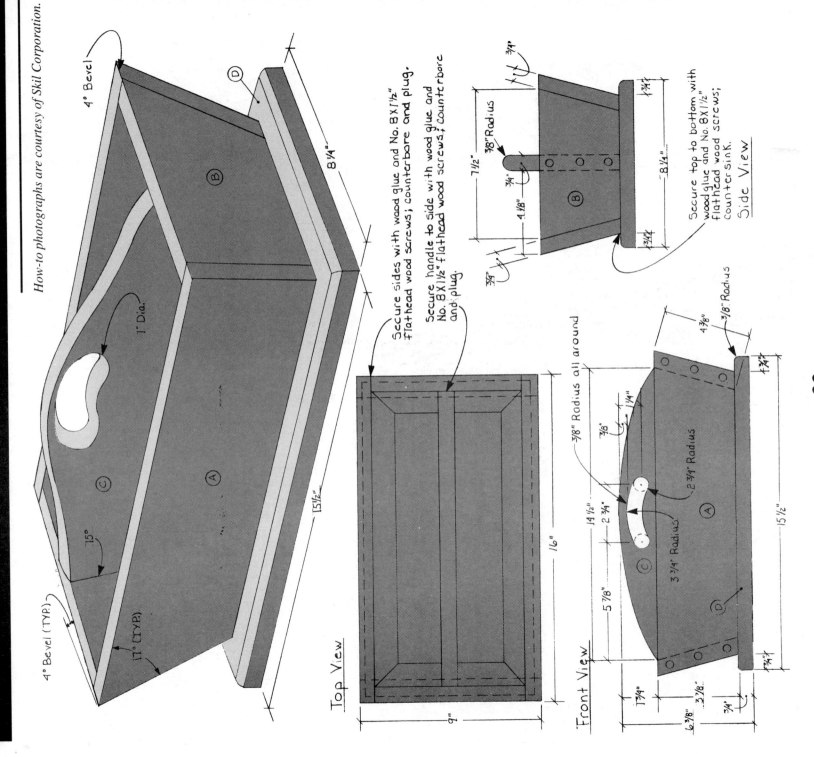

4° Bevel

8¼"

D

1" Dia.

B

C

A

15°

15½"

17° (TYP.)

4° Bevel (TYP.)

16"

9"

Top View

Secure sides with wood glue and No. 8X1½" flathead wood screws; counterbore and plug.

Secure handle to side with wood glue and No. 8X1½" flathead wood screws; counterbore and plug.

¾"

38" Radius

7½"

4⅛"

¾"

B

¾"

¾"

8¼"

1¾"

Secure top to bottom with wood glue and No. 8X1½" flathead wood screws; countersink.

Side View

3/8" Radius all around

4⅜"

3/8" Radius

3/8"

¼"

1¾"

2¾"

14½"

2 ¾" Radius

A

C

D

5⅞"

3 ¾" Radius

6⅜"

3⅜"

¾"

1¾"

¾"

15½"

Front View

32

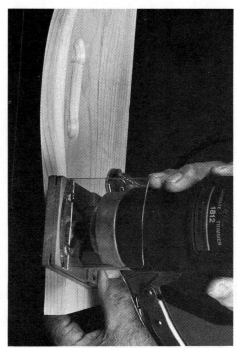

Figure 8.

Carefully round over the top edges for the handle (C) with a router bit installed in your router table.

FINISHING. Finish sand the entire project, then apply a good sealer coat.

Apply a decorative design with stencils or with paints. We used a tole painting design.

When the paint has dried, give the project a coat of satin polyurethane. One additional coat may be required. When sanding between coats, be careful not to sand the design.

❖

Cutting List

A	Side	3/4 x 43/8 x 16	2
B	Side	3/4 x 43/8 x 71/2	2
C	Handle	3/4 x 55/8 x 141/2	1
D	Bottom	3/4 x 81/4 x 151/2	1

Note: All material is pine unless otherwise indicated. All dimensions are in inches.

Figure 9.

Front pattern; each square = 1/2 inch.

Corner Cabinet

A corner cabinet makes use of what is ordinarily wasted space. Our corner cabinet design provides lots of room for displaying china or crystal. Behind the attractive doors you will find more space for storing linens and silverware. For the living room, the corner cabinet offers a place for displaying books and knickknacks, plus a concealed storage area for such items as magazines and videotapes.

SKILL LEVEL. Both intermediate-level and advanced woodworkers will enjoy working on the corner cabinet.

TIPS. The corner cabinet will be attractive no matter what materials are used to build it. Use knotty No. 2 pine or select pine for a classic Colonial look, or use oak for a more stately appearance.

CONSTRUCTION AND ASSEMBLY. Carefully select the narrower pieces that will need to be edge-glued in order to form the shelves (B) and the top (C). A stationary jointer is the best tool for jointing the edges of the wood. Use a good carpenter's glue for the joints, and cover your workbench with plenty of newspaper to keep the surface clean. Apply light clamping pressure, and keep the surface of the wood on a flat plane to prevent warping.

Make use of wasted space by building this practical yet beautiful corner cabinet.

Set your table saw to cut a 45 degree miter, then rip both edges of each side workpiece (A). Now, install a dado blade in your table saw and cut ¾ in. wide by ¼ in. deep dadoes and rabbets into each of the sides (A) to accommodate the shelves (B). Clean out the milled areas with a sharp wood chisel.

Attach the two sides to one another with carpenter's glue and 4d finishing nails. Sink all nailheads. Now, custom cut each of the five shelves (B) so they will fit into the dadoes and rabbets of the two sides. Make sure that the shelves are absolutely flush with the front edge of the unit. When these workpieces are positioned precisely, secure them with carpenter's glue and 4d finishing nails.

Pay particular attention to the cabinet stiles (D) and the top and bottom rails (E, F). The cabinet stiles must protrude beyond the edge of the main cabinet so that the stiles themselves will come in contact with the corner walls. This detail ensures that the unit will fit into a corner that is not square. You will probably need to custom cut the lower portion of the stile to fit over your floor's baseboard.

When the stiles and rails are perfect, lay out the design in the top rail (E) and cut it out on your saber saw. Next, use a small drum sander to finish sand the surface of the wood to a smooth contour.

Corner Cabinet

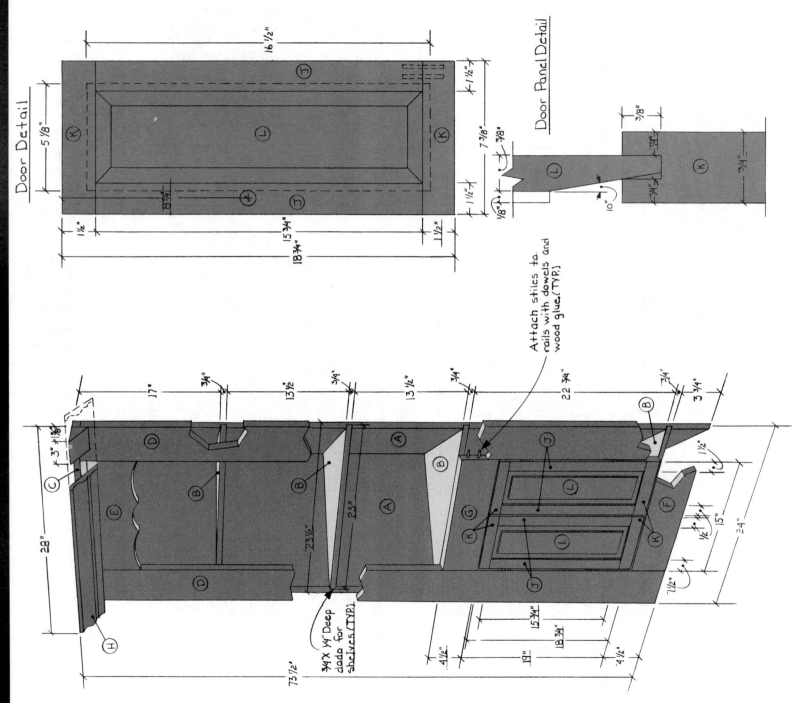

Door Detail

16 1/2"
5 8"
1 1/2"
7 3/8"
3/8"
1 1/2"
18 3/4"
15 3/4"
1/2"
1/2"
1 1/2"

Door Panel Detail

3/8"
1/4"
3/4"
1/8"
10°

K L J

Attach stiles to
rails with dowels and
wood glue.(TYP.)

3/4 X 1/4" Deep
dado for
shelves.(TYP.)

28"
75 1/2"
3"
17"
3/4"
13 1/2"
3/4"
13 1/2"
3/4"
22 3/4"
3/4"
3 3/4"
23 1/2"
23"
1/2"
1"
4 1/2"
19"
15 3/4"
18 3/4"
4 1/2"
7 1/2"
1/2"
1 1/2"
15"

A B C D E F G H J K L

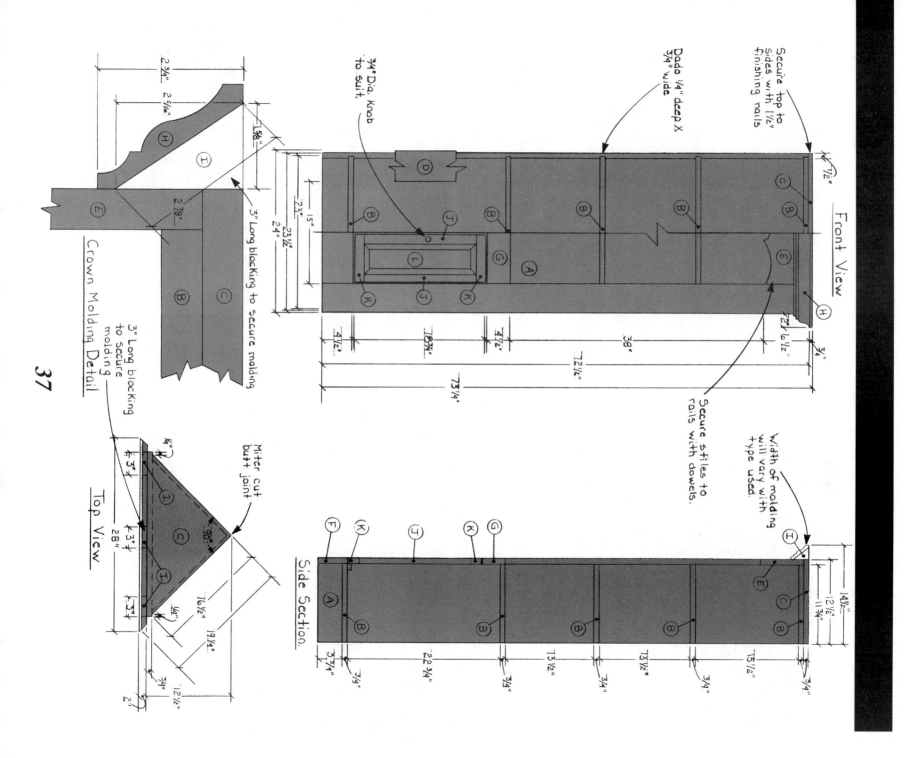

Front View

Secure top to sides with 1½" finishing nails

¾" Dia. Knob to suit.

Dado ¼" deep X ¾" wide

Secure stiles to rails with dowels.

Width of molding will vary with type used.

1½"
2¾"
2⁵⁄₁₆"
2⅞"

H
I
E
B
C

3" Long blocking to secure molding

Crown Molding Detail

15"
23"
23½"
24"

D
B
J
B
B
B
B
C
A
G
L
E
K
J
K
H

½"
4½"
4½"
18¾"
6½"
¾"
38"
72½"
73¼"
2½"

Top View

3" Long blocking to secure molding

Miter cut butt joint

¼"
3"
3"
3"
28"
90°
16½"
19¼"
¼"
12½"
¾"
2"

I
C
I

Side Section

F
K
J
K
G
A
B
B
B
B
H
E
C

14½"
12½"
11¾"
3¾"
⅜"
22¾"
¾"
13½"
¾"
13½"
¾"
15½"
¾"

37

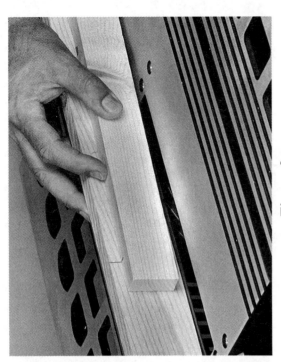

Figure 1.

The side workpieces (A) have 45 degree bevels. For accurate cuts, rip the workpiece to its proper width before cutting the edge to a 45 degree angle, as we are doing here.

Figure 2.

Cut a stopped groove into each of the door rails (K). Use guide marks on your saw's fence to determine the starting and stopping points. Square the cut with a wood chisel.

Figure 3.

Form the raised door panels (L) by setting your saw blade to cut the panel's beveled edge. Make a test cut in scrap material before you work on the actual project. Then cut the bevel into each of the four edges, making sure that the panel rests snugly against the fence and that your fingers are well out of harm's way.

Figure 4.

Readjust the table saw blade to cut 1/8 in. deep and to meet the bevel that you previously cut into the door panel.

Figure 5.
Add a nice detail to the stile (D) by squaring the beveled edge with a portable power plane. Form a flat plane approximately 1/8 in. wide.

Figure 6.
Use a palm sander to sand the bevel. Be careful not to dig into the protruding edge of the raised panel. Apply light sanding pressure while making long strokes to avoid gouging the bevel.

Cutting List

Note: All material is pine unless otherwise indicated. All dimensions are in inches.

A	Side	1/2 x 16 1/2 x 72 1/2 plywood	2
B	Shelf	3/4 x 16 x 23	5
C	Top	3/4 x 17 1/4 x 17 1/4	1
D	Stile	3/4 x 4 1/2 x 72 1/2	2
E	Top rail	3/4 x 6 1/2 x 15	1
F	Bottom rail	3/4 x 4 1/2 x 15	1
G	Middle rail	3/4 x 4 1/2 x 15	1
H	Crown molding	11/16 x 2 3/4 x 28	1
I	Securing blocks	1 5/8 x 27/8 x 3	3
J	Door stile	3/4 x 1 1/2 x 15 3/4	4
K	Door rail	3/4 x 1 1/2 x 7 3/8	4
L	Door panel	1/2 x 5 5/8 x 16 1/2	2

Now, join the top rail (E), middle rail (G) and bottom rail (F) to each stile (D) with the aid of a plate joiner or a doweling jig. Dry-assemble the stiles and rails onto the cabinet face and check to make sure that they fit precisely. Once you are satisfied with the fit, attach the stiles and rails to one another using carpenter's glue and your chosen joining material (either wafers or dowels). While the glue is still wet, set the stile and rail frame onto the face of the cabinet and secure it to the cabinet with carpenter's glue and 4d finishing nails. If necessary, use bar clamps to keep the joints tight. Allow the glue to cure before moving the cabinet.

39

CUTTING CROWN MOLDING

Figure 7.

In order to cut the crown molding (H), set your power miter saw 45 degrees right of center and position the molding as shown. Carefully make your cut.

DOORS. Carefully measure the cabinet's door cavity, and then cut the door stiles (J) and the door rails (K) to suit. Using a dado blade on your table saw, cut a ¼ in. wide by ⅜ in. deep groove along the full length of each door rail. It is imperative that the groove be precisely in the middle of the edge. We recommend that you make several practice cuts using scrap material first.

Now, cut the stopped grooves into each of the four door rails, and square the cuts with a sharp wood chisel. As always, clamp the workpiece securely to the workbench while squaring the cut.

Carefully cut out each of the door panels (L), and then set your saw to cut the bevels. You will need to cut into scrap material first in order to determine the proper height of the cuts. Then cut each of the edges of the door panels on your table saw. Follow this process by readjusting the table saw blade to cut square at a height of ⅛ inch. Then readjust the fence so the blade will meet the beveled cut that you just made. As you make each cut, the panel will start to take form.

Finish sand the beveled edges of both door panels with a palm sander. Sand in long strokes, and periodically check each panel to see how it fits within the door stiles and rails. When everything is perfect, secure the door stiles and rails to one another with carpenter's glue and dowels. Also, insert the door panels, but do not glue them into place yet. The door panels must be allowed to float within the door frame. For tight joints, use a bar clamp to apply light pressure.

Mortise the areas for the door hinges on the cabinet frame. Install two magnetic latches inside the bottom shelf to act as door stops. Then drill holes for the knobs and install the hardware.

CROWN MOLDING. Crown molding is readily available at most home centers and lumberyards. We do not recommend making your own crown molding.

It is quite easy to ruin a piece of crown molding when making a cut, because the molding is often cut at compound angles. The ideal cutting tool is a power miter saw. It allows you to place the molding so that it is at the actual angle at which it will be installed. The most difficult part is determining if you have

Figure 8.
Move the crown molding (H) to the cabinet to make sure it is cut at the proper angle. Then determine where the other angle should be cut.

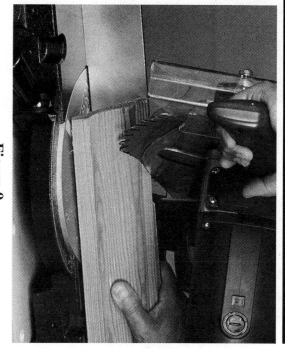

Figure 9.
Readjust the power miter saw to cut 45 degrees left of center and reposition the crown molding (H) for cutting. Make your cut a little longer just in case your mark was off. Test-fit this workpiece, and then make light cuts as needed until the crown molding is at its exact length.

made the cut at the proper angle. We recommend that you buy about 6 to 10 in. of extra length to allow for any errors.

Make one cut at one end of the crown molding. Then test-fit the molding to the corner cabinet to determine if it is in fact cut at the proper angle. If so, reset the power miter saw to cut 45 degrees on the other side of center, and locate the precise starting point on the crown molding so that the molding will be flush with the mitered edges of the cabinet stiles (D). Once you have determined the starting point, cut about ⅛ in. long and then test the molding. You can always trim off ⅟₁₆ in. at a time until the crown molding is perfect, but you can never add to the length. With a little bit of patience, you will be satisfied with the result of your efforts.

Now, custom cut the securing blocks (I) to help support the crown molding. Cut three or four of these blocks, and attach them to the upper portion of the cabinet with carpenter's glue and finishing nails. Be sure to predrill the nail holes to avoid splitting. After the glue has dried thoroughly, attach the crown molding with glue and 4d finishing nails.

FINISHING. Remove the door hardware as well as the magnetic latches inside the cabinet, and sink all nailheads with a nail set. Fill in any blemishes with a good nontoxic wood filler. Follow this up with a thorough sanding of all of the cabinet parts. Remove any dust particles with a damp (but not wet), clean cloth.

Deciding what kind of finish to apply is the tough part. On this project we used an antique application.

❖

Wall Display Unit

ost of us have special mementos that we have collected over the years: a porcelain cup and saucer, a silver baby spoon, our great-grandfather's gold watch, antique salt and pepper shakers — the list goes on. This wall unit is just the ticket for displaying those treasured items. The three drawers at the bottom of the unit are perfect for storing small treasures, or you may want to line one of the drawers with a plastic dish and put in a trailing ivy vine.

Our detailed construction techniques help make this project go together smoothly. Though we used polyurethane on our wall unit, try painting the unit to match your decor and adding stenciling or rosemaling accents for a rustic look. Whatever finish you choose, we are sure you will find that this wall unit can suit a multitude of purposes in just about any room in the house.

SKILL LEVEL. This project is suitable for beginning or intermediate woodworkers. The project is simple to build, but the techniques used to sand and finish the project will determine the success of the final product.

TIPS. Take your time when making each joint, ensuring that all joints are nice and tight. Any gaps

Display your knickknacks and miniature valuables attractively and safely with this sturdy wall unit.

will be quite noticeable on this small project. Then finish sand until you achieve a mirrorlike finish. Apply a sample finish to scrap material first to make absolutely certain that the finish is what you want; don't be satisfied with a merely okay appearance.

CONSTRUCTION. Cut out all of the project parts with the exception of the drawer parts and the plywood backs. Use a table saw equipped with a planer blade. This type of saw blade provides an ultrasmooth finish that minimizes sanding.

Using a router equipped with a 3/8 in. rounding over bit with pilot, carefully rout the top/bottom/middle work-pieces (E). Move the router counterclockwise when making these cuts, and make sure to use a sharp bit so the wood will not be marred with burn marks, which are difficult to remove.

Next, equip your table saw with a dado blade set to a 3/4 in. width and a 3/8 in. height. Carefully lay out the dado positions in both side workpieces (A). Make a test cut and check to ensure that the display shelves (G) fit snugly into the dado. After you are satisfied with the adjustments, make each of the cuts using your saw's miter gauge.

Use a sharp wood chisel to clean out the dadoes that you cut into the side workpieces. Make sure that

43

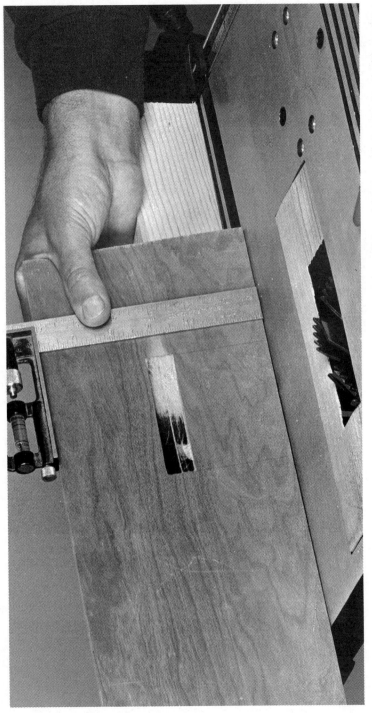

Figure 1.

The middle and bottom workpieces (E) require stopped rabbets. Here we show a rabbet cut set at the proper depth and height on a piece of scrap material. In order to mark the proper location on your table saw, use a carpenter's square to determine the starting point on the flat part of the workpiece.

you clamp each workpiece to your workbench to prevent accidents.

Readjust your dado blade to cut rabbets to accommodate the two shelves (F). Cut these rabbets into the two sides that you just dadoed.

Also, cut rabbets into the back edges of the top and bottom side workpieces (A, B), as well as the middle and bottom workpieces (E). Pay particular attention to the top/bottom/middle workpieces, because they require stopped rabbets. If the rabbets were to continue the full length of the material, they would show at the time of assembly. Before cutting, you need to locate starting and stopping points on your table saw.

Figure 2.

With the table saw blade turned off, lock the test work-piece onto the blade so that it is at the location to begin the stopped rabbet. Project the mark where the rabbet begins onto the fence. Use a similar procedure for determining the stopping points.

44

ASSEMBLY. Begin assembly with the upper shelf unit. Glue the shelves (F, G) into the two top side workpieces (A). Make sure that the three display

---

Begin cutting the stopped rabbet into the middle workpiece (E) by aligning the start marks on your workpiece with the start marks on the fence. Then carefully move the workpiece down into the rotating blade. Make sure that you have a firm grip on the material and that your fingers are well away from the blade.

This is best accomplished by making test cuts in scrap material.

Some novice woodworkers will make the mistake of sanding the project parts at this point, prior to assembling the project. Although it is easier to sand the project parts before assembly, this can result in thinner shelves that fit loosely in the dadoes. Consequently, the unit will have unsightly gaps and will not hold up.

Figure 3.

---

shelves (G) are flush with the outside edge. If they are not, the back (C) will not fit properly. Use bar clamps to secure the assembly and a carpenter's square to ensure that the unit is absolutely square. Allow the glue to cure for 24 hours.

Assemble the lower unit by gluing the bottom sides (B) and the dividers (H) to the bottom and middle workpieces (E). Again, use carpenter's glue and a combination square to make sure that the unit is square. Clamp the assembly.

Cutting List

A	Top side	¾ x 5¼ x 18¼	2
B	Bottom side	¾ x 5¼ x 4	2
C	Back	¼ x 17¼ x 17½ plywood	2
D	Back	¼ x 7¼ x 4¾ plywood	1
E	Top/bottom/ middle	¾ x 6 x 20	3
F	Shelf	¾ x 5¼ x 17¼	2
G	Display shelf	¾ x 5 x 17¼	3
H	Divider	¾ x 5 x 4	2
I	Drawer front	¾ x 3¹⁵/₁₆ x 4⅞	3
J	Drawer back	½ x 3¹⁵/₁₆ x 4⅞	3
K	Drawer side	½ x 3¹⁵/₁₆ x 4⅜	6
L	Drawer bottom	¼ x 4⅜ x 4⅜ plywood	3

Note: All material is cherry unless otherwise indicated. All dimensions are in inches.

This project is courtesy of the American Plywood Association, P.O. Box 11700, Tacoma, WA 98411. How-to photographs are courtesy of Skil Corporation.

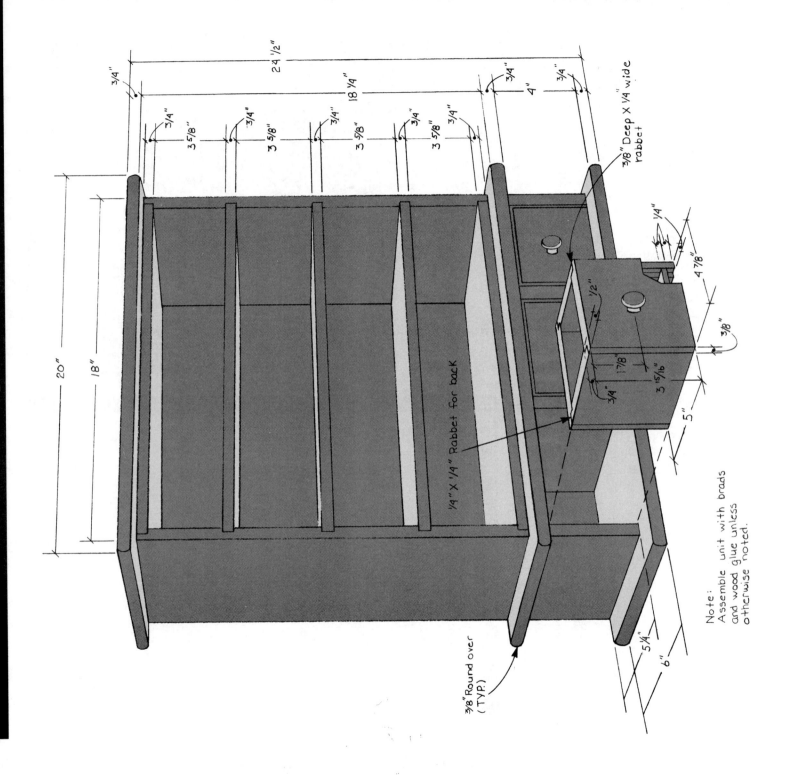

24 1/2"

18 1/4"

3/4"

3/4"   3/4"   3/4"   3/4"

3 5/8"   3 5/8"   3 5/8"   3 5/8"

3/4"   3/4"

4"

3/8" Deep X 1/4 wide rabbet

1/4"

4 7/8"

1/2"

3/8"

20"

18"

1 7/8"

3 15/16"

3/4"

5"

1/4" X 1/4" Rabbet for back

5 1/4"

6"

3/8" Round over (Typ.)

Note:
Assemble unit with brads
and wood glue unless
otherwise noted.

46

When the glue in both the upper and the lower units has cured, glue the two units together with carpenter's glue and then clamp securely. Similarly, glue and clamp the top (E). While the glue is drying, carefully measure the inside cavities of the drawers to ensure that they are precisely 5 in. wide.

The drawers slide on the bottom workpiece (E) and incorporate a 1/16 in. gap on the top and to the left and right of each drawer. Following the dimensions on the drawing carefully, cut out each of the drawer parts to their precise widths and lengths. Then set up your table saw to create the appropriate rabbets in each of the drawer parts (I, J, K). When making these types of cuts, it is imperative that you first make test cuts in

scrap material until you are satisfied with the results. After making the finish cuts in each of the drawer workpieces, smooth the rabbet cuts with a sharp wood chisel.

Next, readjust the dado blade to groove each of the drawer workpieces to accommodate the drawer bottoms (L).

Dry-assemble each drawer unit, making sure that all the joints are perfect. Then glue the drawer workpieces together and secure them in place with a band clamp. Do not glue the drawer bottoms in place at this time.

Custom cut the backs (C, D) and install to the project with carpenter's glue and brads.

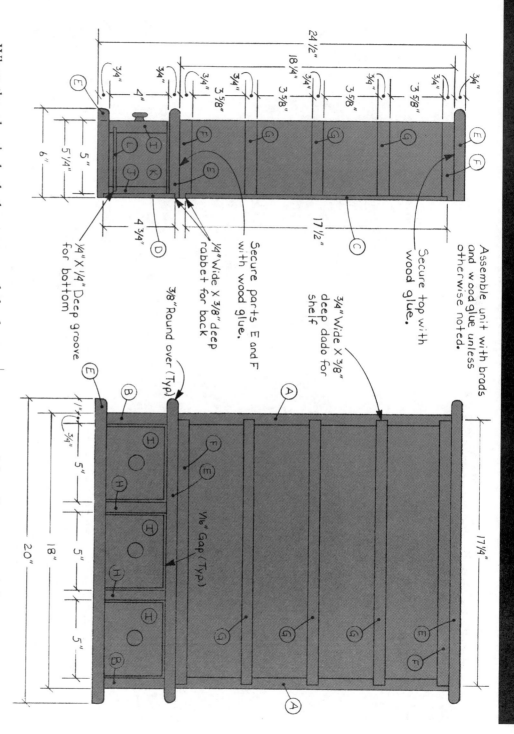

Assemble unit with brads and wood glue unless otherwise noted.

Secure top with wood glue.

3/4" Wide X 3/8" deep dado for shelf

Secure parts E and F with wood glue.

1/4" Wide X 3/8" deep rabbet for back

3/8" Round over (Typ)

1/4" X 1/4" Deep groove for bottom

1/16" Gap (Typ)

Wall Display Unit

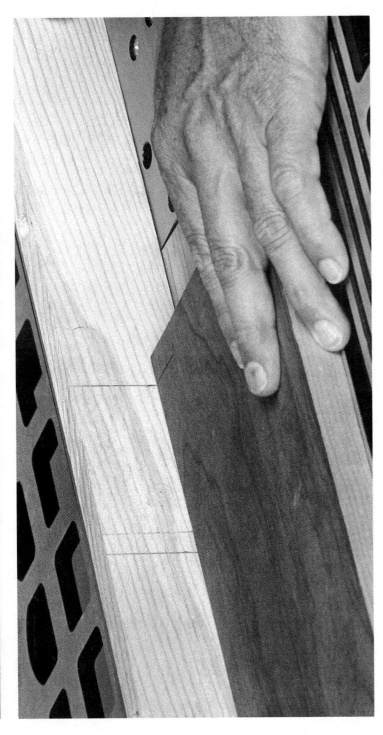

Figure 4.

As you move the workpiece forward to finish the stopped rabbet, stop at the point where the stop marks on your workpiece coincide with the stop mark on the fence. When you have reached this point, stop the table saw and remove the workpiece from the fence.

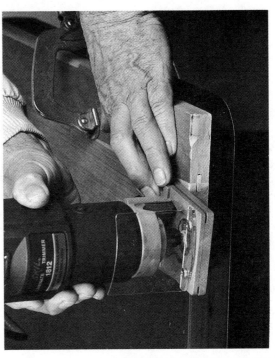

Figure 5.

The top/bottom/middle workpieces (E) require rounding over on three edges. Here we laid out the top workpiece (E) and routed the top edge as shown. This will prevent wood splintering, which can easily occur when routing cross grain.

Carefully locate the positions of each of the drawer knobs and drill appropriately sized holes for accommodating the knob screws.

FINISHING. Finish sand the entire project and dull all showing edges. Apply a sanding sealer and allow it to dry thoroughly. Then give it a light sanding.

We used a satin finish polyurethane on our project. Whichever finish you choose, be sure to apply it in a dust-free environment. Complete the project by installing the knobs. Mount the unit to the wall with two No. 10 by 2 in. flathead wood screws. Make sure that you countersink the wood screws, and drive them into solid wood or wall studs.

❖

48

Figure 6.

Now, we complete the routing of the top workpiece (E) by moving the router counterclockwise. Because we are moving the router counterclockwise and into the remaining edge, we first back-cut into the area indicated with an arrow; otherwise the wood's edge will split.

Kitchen Helpers

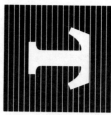

he efficient cook knows that time is wasted when supplies and utensils are scattered all over the kitchen. These two colorful niches — a food-wrap holder and a cookbook/recipe holder — pull together related items and keep them handy. Each project is so easy and economical to build that you will probably want to make them both. We painted these niches blue to contrast with our decor. Built of oak or ash, they are an especially handsome addition to any kitchen.

SKILL LEVEL. Both projects are quite suitable for beginning woodworkers and can be constructed with basic hand tools if desired.

TIPS. Use aerosol spray paint to finish these projects. Paintbrushes do not do a good job inside tight areas, such as the cavity for the food-wrap holder and the door cavity of the cookbook/recipe holder.

CONSTRUCTION. Carefully lay out all of the project parts on plywood (with the exception of workpieces D and E). Use a carpenter's square and a compass to make the layouts and to locate the center lines.

Lay out the two dowel covers (D) on hardboard that is approximately 6 in. square. Draw the perime-

Make cooking a pleasure and keep your kitchen neat with these handy kitchen helpers.

ters with a compass. The extra material allows you to safely cut out the disks with a scroll saw and safeguards getting your fingers too close to the unforgiving blade. Now, cut out the two disks.

Cut the remaining project parts to their overall lengths and widths. Use a scroll saw to cut curves into the food-wrap holder's side workpieces (A). Drill the required holes for the dowel into the side workpieces (A).

Sand the edges of the plywood with a disk sander equipped with fine grit sandpaper. Follow this up by sanding the surfaces of all of the project parts with a pad sander or a palm sander.

ASSEMBLY. Assemble both projects using carpenter's glue and 4d finishing nails.

Begin with the food-wrap holder by assembling the top (B) and the shelf (C) to the two sides (A). In a similar manner, assemble the cookbook/recipe holder by attaching the shelves (BB) and the divider (CC) to the two sides (AA). Square the assembly by installing the back (DD).

Next, attach the two drawer fronts (FF) and the backs (GG) to the two drawer sides (EE). Square the assembly by installing the two drawer bottoms (HH).

Once the glue has cured, sand the two dowel covers (D) for the food-wrap holder. Glue only one of

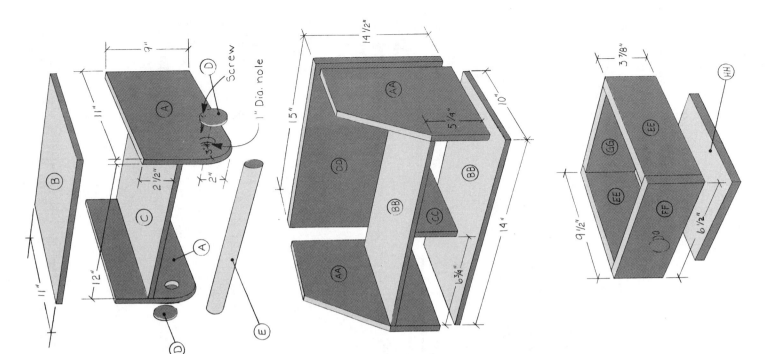

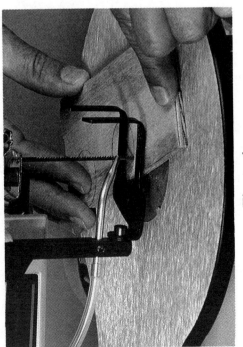

Figure 1.

Draw the circles for the two dowel covers (D) onto an oversize sheet of hardboard or thin plywood. Then cut out the perimeters with a scroll saw or a jigsaw. This makes the process of cutting out the disks safer.

Figure 2.

Use a stationary disk sander to smooth the plywood edges.

the dowel covers to the unit. Predrill a hole for a ³⁄₈ in. long flathead wood screw. Countersink the hole.

In order to mount the food-wrap holder, you will need to predrill four fastener holes into the two sides (A). (You may be able to drive shorter wood screws through the shelf and into the unit.) To make the fastener holes, use a drill to bore at approximately 60

Figure 3.

Predrill holes for attaching the food-wrap holder to a kitchen cabinet. Once the unit is assembled, drill a pilot hole as shown at approximately a 60 degree angle and up 3/4 in. from the edge. Follow this up by countersinking the hole so that the wood screw will not protrude from the edge of the project.

degrees, up ¾ in. from the edge. Drill the four holes, making sure they miss the nails that you used to fasten the sides to the top. Carefully countersink each of the four holes.

We recommend finishing the projects with aerosol spray paint. Choose an appropriate sealer and spray all of the project parts in a well-ventilated area. Make sure to wear a mask and goggles. When the projects are dry, lightly sand the sealer and apply the paint of your choice. You may have to apply two to four coats, sanding lightly between each coat.

FINISHING. Make sure that you dull all showing edges and fill in all blemishes with a suitable wood filler. Finish sand all of the project parts and remove fine dust particles with a damp, clean cloth.

MOUNTING. Mount the food-wrap holder underneath a kitchen cabinet using four No. 8 by 1½ in. flathead wood screws. Depending on the thickness of

the material that you are driving into, you may have to use shorter wood screws. Note that you may be able to drive shorter wood screws through the shelf and into the unit.

Slip a new roll of paper towels onto the dowel (E). Attach the dowel cover (D) to secure the paper towels. To add a new roll of papers towels, simply twist the cover to remove the dowel.

For the cookbook/recipe holder, drill holes for the drawer pulls into the drawer fronts (FF) and install.

This project is courtesy of Georgia-Pacific Corporation, 133 Peachtree St. N.E., P.O. Box 105605, Atlanta, GA 30348.
How-to photographs are courtesy of Skil Corporation.

Cutting List

Food-Wrap Holder

A	Side	½ x 9 x 11	2
B	Top	½ x 11 x 13	1
C	Shelf	½ x 11 x 12	1
D	Dowel cover	⅛ x 1½ x 1½ hardboard	2
E	Dowel	1 dia. x 13 hardwood	1

Cookbook/Recipe Holder

AA	Side	½ x 10 x 14½	2
BB	Shelf	½ x 10 x 14	2
CC	Divider	½ x 4 x 10	1
DD	Back	½ x 14½ x 15	1
EE	Drawer side	½ x 3⅞ x 9½	4
FF	Drawer front	½ x 3⅞ x 6½	2
GG	Drawer back	½ x 3⅞ x 5½	2
HH	Drawer bottom	½ x 5½ x 9	2

Note: All material is plywood unless otherwise indicated. All dimensions are in inches.

Workbench

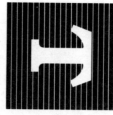

his hardworking workbench is every woodworker's dream. It provides loads of work room, with a surface that is more than 8 ft. long, plus tons of storage space that will keep your tools safe and organized. Best of all, you can build it yourself, using a minimum of time and money.

SKILL LEVEL. This is a good project for intermediate-level woodworkers.

TIPS. Hold off on cutting all of the project parts to their overall widths and lengths. Instead, cut the materials that you need for each phase of assembly. Today's dimensional lumber may be a little thicker or a little wider than you expect, which could easily result in unsightly gaps when you put everything together.

CONSTRUCTION.

Begin by cutting the legs (H, I) to length. Next, cut the top side rails (D), the top front/middle/back rails (C), the bottom side rails (G), the bottom back rail (E) and the bottom front rail (F). Cut a rabbet into the bottom edges of the top middle/back rails (C).

Assemble this unit minus the top front rail (C) using carpenter's glue, along with both ¼ in. by 2 in. lag screws and ¼ in. by 2¾ in. carriage bolts with flat

The workbench. Every shop needs one — can't function without it. Now you can build your own.

workbench top to hold the top (A) in position. Attach the cleats with carpenter's glue and 1 in. drywall screws. Then cut the top (A) and secure it to the cleats with 1 in. drywall screws. Do not use glue. If the top requires replacement, this will allow you to detach it easily.

Cut the cleats (P, Q, R, S, V), and attach them inside the top front rail (C) in position and secure with glue and drywall screws. Then custom cut the top center front rail (T), the top center back rail (U), the dividers (L), the side bottoms (J), the shelf (M) and the middle bottom (K). After you have custom cut these workpieces, install them with carpenter's glue and drywall nails. Note that you will have to notch the dividers (L) to fit around the underside of the workbench top.

Now, install the remaining top front rail (C) in position and secure with glue and drywall screws. Then custom cut the top center front rail (T), the top center back rail (U), the dividers (L), the side bottoms (J), the shelf (M) and the middle bottom (K). After you have custom cut these workpieces, install them with carpenter's glue and drywall nails. Note that you will have to notch the dividers (L) to fit around the underside of the workbench top.

Custom cut the tray bottom (B) from waferboard and secure it in place with carpenter's glue and finishing nails.

washers. Follow the illustration to determine where the carriage bolts are located. Be sure to predrill the holes for both the lag screws and the carriage bolts. Square the assembly, and allow the glue to dry for 24 hours.

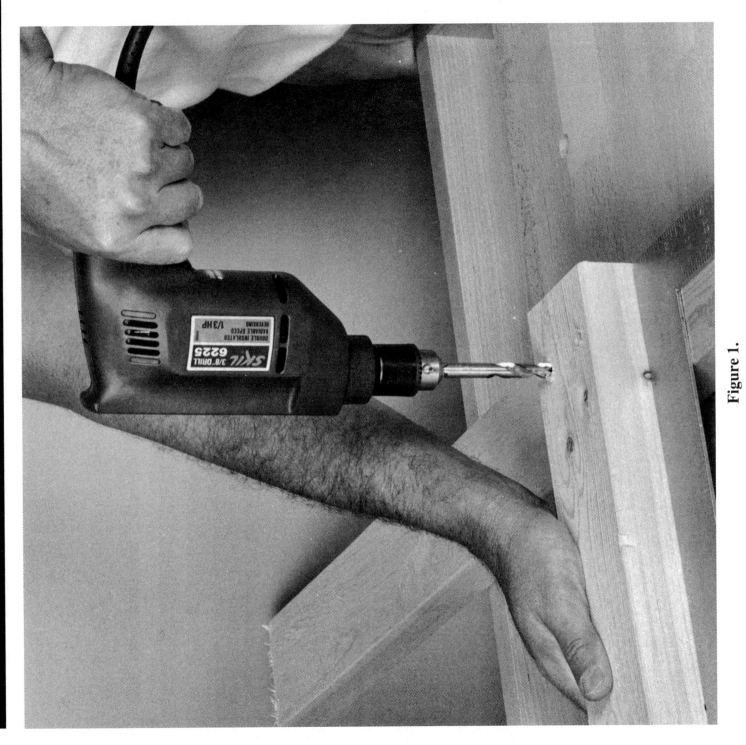

Figure 1.

Drill two holes for securing the bottom front rail (F) to the front legs (H). These holes will accommodate the carriage bolts.

56

Cutting List

A	Top	3/4 x 21 1/2 x 96 waferboard	1
B	Tray bottom	1/2 x 7 x 96 3/4 plywood or waferboard	1
C	Top front/middle /back rail	3/4 x 5 1/2 x 96	3
D	Top side rail	3/4 x 5 1/2 x 30	2
E	Bottom back rail	3/4 x 3 1/2 x 96	1
F	Bottom front rail	3/4 x 3 1/2 x 96	1
G	Bottom side rail	3/4 x 3 1/2 x 69 1/4	1
H	Front leg	1 1/2 x 3 1/2 x 28 1/2	3
I	Back leg	1 1/2 x 3 1/2 x 33 1/4	3
J	Side bottom	1 1/2 x 3 1/2 x 34	3
K	Middle bottom	3/4 x 20 1/4 x 29 1/4	2
L	Divider	3/4 x 21 x 29 1/4	2
M	Shelf	3/4 x 20 3/4 x 29 1/4 waferboard	1
N	Door	3/4 x 11 1/8 x 18 1/2	4
O	Door handle	3/4 x 1 1/2 x 9 5/8	2
P	Back cleat	3/4 x 1 x 30 1/4	1
Q	Front cleat	3/4 x 1 x 64 1/2	1
R	Front cleat	3/4 x 1 x 25 1/4	1
S	Side cleat	3/4 x 1 x 16 1/2	2
T	Top center front rail	3/4 x 4 3/4 x 21	1
U	Top center back rail	3/4 x 5 x 6 1/4	1
V	Back cleat	3/4 x 1 x 65 1/4	1

Note: All material is pine unless otherwise indicated. All dimensions are in inches.

Custom cut the doors (N) and door handles (O). Then bevel the edges of the door on your table saw. Afterward, attach the door handles to the door with carpenter's glue and 1 1/4 in. drywall screws. Now, hinge the doors to the workbench.

FINISHING. Fill in any dents or recesses with a nontoxic wood filler, then sand the entire project.

Apply a sanding sealer and allow the project to dry thoroughly before sanding it with a pad sander. Follow this up with an application of a low gloss polyurethane finish.

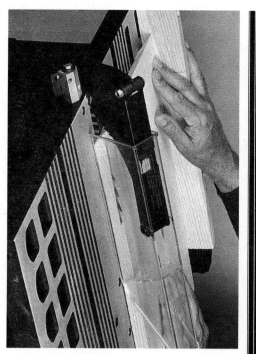

Figure 2.

Bevel the doors (N) on your table saw. Use a miter gauge for cutting the bevels into the narrower widths, and then cut the longer bevels as shown.

❖

This project is courtesy of Georgia-Pacific Corporation, 133 Peachtree St. N.E., P.O. Box 105605, Atlanta, GA 30348. How-to photographs are courtesy of Skil Corporation.

Workbench

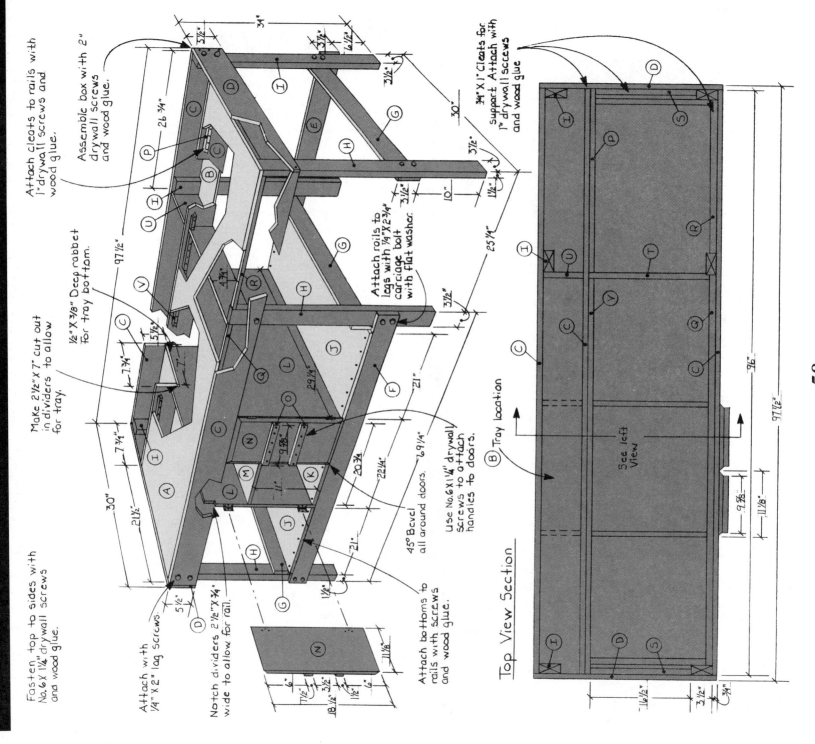

Make 2½" x 7" cut out in dividers to allow for tray.

Fasten top to sides with No.6x1¼" drywall screws and wood glue.

Attach with ¼" x 2" lag screws.

Notch dividers 2½"x ¾" wide to allow for rail.

Attach bottoms to rails with screws and wood glue.

Attach cleats to rails with 1" drywall screws and wood glue.

Assemble box with 2" drywall screws and wood glue.

½"x ⅜" Deep rabbet for tray bottom.

Attach legs to rails with ¼"x 2¾" carriage bolt with flat washer.

45° Bevel all around doors.

Use No.6x1¼" drywall screws to attach handles to doors.

Attach cleats for support. Attach with 1" drywall screws and wood glue.

¾"x 1" Cleats for support. Attach with 1" drywall screws and wood glue.

Tray location

See left View

Top View Section

58

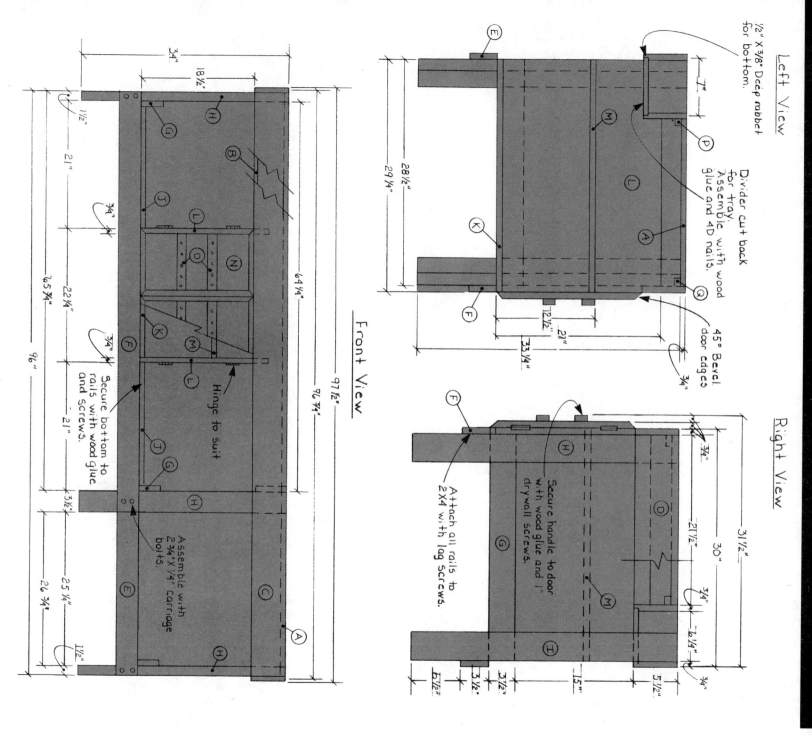

Left View

½" X ⅜" Deep rabbet
for bottom.

Front View

Divider cut back
for tray.
Assemble with wood
glue and 4D nails.

Right View

45° Bevel
door edges

Hinge to suit

Secure bottom to
rails with wood glue
and screws.

Assemble with
2¾" X ¼" carriage
bolts.

Attach all rails to
2X4 with lag screws.

Secure handle to door
with wood glue and 1"
drywall screws.

59

Lap Desk

his wonderful lap desk allows you to pay bills or write letters without leaving the comfort of your couch or favorite chair. The hinged lid hides a roomy area for storing stationery, envelopes, stamps and the like. The special wells at the top of the desk can hold letters, pencils, pens, paper clips, a stapler and tape. Everything you need for all your correspondence is at hand with this lap desk. It is the next best thing to having your very own personal secretary!

SKILL LEVEL. This is a good project for intermediate-level woodworkers who are good at joining.

TIPS. The project calls for assembling the joints with dowels. However, you can substitute counterbored wood screws for the dowels, covering the recesses with wood plugs. This is a simpler technique and it would lend individuality to the project.

CONSTRUCTION. Carefully lay out all of the project parts on walnut material except the plywood bottom (B). You may have to edge-glue several narrower pieces to form the top (A). If you have to edge-glue, make sure that you use a portable plane and do not allow any gaps between the seams.

Next, cut out all of the project parts, including the plywood bottom (B), on your table saw. Groove the

The rich look of walnut enhances this very practical, highly functional lap desk.

total length of the back (D) to accommodate the plywood bottom. You also will have to cut stopped grooves into the sides (C) and the front (E). Once you have cut out the stopped dadoes on your table saw, square the cuts with a wood chisel.

Round over the two front edges of the side workpieces (C). Use a rounding over bit equipped with a pilot guide on your router, or round over the edge on a router table. Cut the bevel in the hinged edge of the top workpiece (A).

Cut mortises into the top's beveled edge to accommodate the 1½ in. hinges.

Carefully lay out the notches to be cut into the two side workpieces (C). It is best to use a band saw with a ½ in. wide blade installed to make these long, straight cuts. When finished, test-fit the sides to the front (E) and lay out the precise bevel for the front workpiece. Then cut the bevel on your table saw. Make sure the front workpiece's beveled edge is flush with the adjoining sides.

Prefinish the plywood bottom (B) with a dark walnut stain. Stain both sides of the plywood. It is easier to finish the workpiece at this stage than at the time of the project's assembly.

ASSEMBLY. Assemble the project using a doweling jig and carpenter's glue. Drill the dowel holes, then assemble the front, back, sides, divider (G) and middle (F), along with the plywood bottom, using

Lap Desk

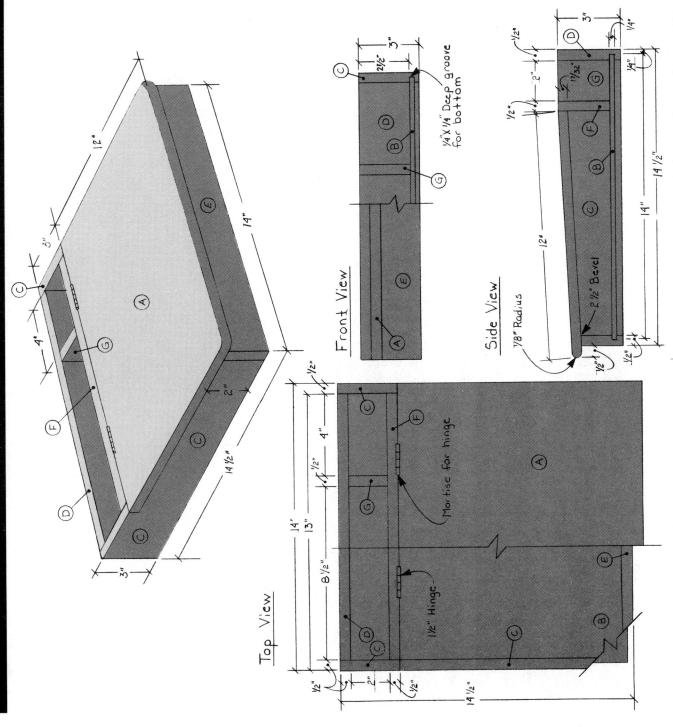

Front View

¼"X¼" Deep groove
for bottom

Side View

2½° Bevel

⅞" Radius

Top View

Mortise for hinge

1½" Hinge

dowels and glue. Use clamps, as well, to keep the assembly square and the joints tight. Allow the glue to dry for 24 hours.

Remove any excess glue with a dull wood chisel and then finish sand the main unit. Be careful not to gouge any of the side workpieces (C), or the top (A) will not rest evenly. During the sanding process, periodically position the top in place to ensure that there are no gaps between the top and the workpieces that it adjoins.

Figure 1.

Cutting List

A	Top	½ x 12 x 14	1
B	Bottom	½ x 13½ x 14	1
		plywood	
C	Side	½ x 3 x 14	2
D	Back	½ x 3 x 13	1
E	Front	½ x 2 x 14	1
F	Middle	½ x 2½ x 13	1
G	Divider	½ x 2½ x 2	1

Note: All material is walnut unless otherwise indicated. All dimensions are in inches.

Cut out the notched area in each of the side workpieces (C) with a band saw. Use a wide cutting blade to help obtain a nice, straight cut. Use the cut side workpieces (C) to determine where the bevel should be cut into the front (E). Then cut the bevel on your table saw.

Next, install the hinges to the top. Connect the hinges to the middle workpiece (F) using the screws supplied with the hinges.

FINISHING. Remove the hinges and finish sand the entire project. Slightly dull all showing edges and finish with a light sandpaper so that the wood is absolutely smooth to the touch.

Apply a coat of sanding sealer to the entire project, including the underside, and allow it to dry. Once the project is dry, give it a light sanding and remove all of the dust particles with a damp cloth.

Apply a satin finish to the project. This coat may be enough, but if desired, apply one more coat. Complete the project by reinstalling the hinges.

How-to photographs are courtesy of Skil Corporation.

Figure 2.

Cut a stopped groove into the front (E) with a dado blade installed in your table saw. Make sure that the workpiece is firmly clamped to the workbench when cutting. Square the groove with a sharp wood chisel.

63

Gateleg Table

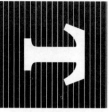

This compact, versatile table can add interest to a room or hall without taking up much space. Folded down, the table is only 12 in. wide. Bring up the table extension, and you have a 24 in. by 36 in. table that is perfect for casual dining. You can also use the table as a refreshment station for entertaining or as an accent piece for displaying knickknacks and photos. Special finishing touches, such as antiquing, add even more elegance to the table.

SKILL LEVEL. This is a good project for beginning woodworkers.

TIPS. It is very important that you buy A-B plywood. This will save on sanding time and help ensure that the project workpieces are nice and straight and free of warping.

CONSTRUCTION AND ASSEMBLY. Cut the tops (D), aprons (A, I) and sides (B) to their overall widths and lengths. Cut them slightly oversize and then joint the edges.

Each of the legs (C) are glued up from thinner workpieces. We selected maple for the legs and ripped the strips approximately ⅜ in. wider than what is called for in the drawing. After surface-gluing the legs and clamping them securely, we allowed the glue to cure

This gateleg table adds an elegant look to any room yet takes up very little space. Best of all, it is easy to build!

for 24 hours. Then we jointed the legs on a stationary jointer until the proper widths were achieved. Finally, each leg was cut to length on a table saw.

Cut out the contours in the apron (A) and the hinged apron (I). Draw the pattern on the nonshowing surface of each of the workpieces using a compass and a yardstick. Then cut each design with a saber saw equipped with a plywood cutting blade. Sand each of the contours using either a drum sander installed in your drill press or a power drill.

Miter the edges of the apron (A) and the two sides (B) on your table saw. Make sure that the joints that are formed produce a perfect 90 degree angle. When everything is perfect, glue and nail the apron to the sides with carpenter's glue and 4d finishing nails. Remember to sink all nailheads. Follow this up by nailing and gluing the top (D) to the apron and the sides.

Now, secure the legs (C) to the top assembly with glue and finishing nails. Clamp four of the legs in place, and then secure the legs by driving finishing nails into the apron and the side workpieces. Allow the glue to cure before moving the assembly.

Similarly, attach the two remaining legs to each of the two hinged aprons. Again, use glue and finishing

Gateleg Table

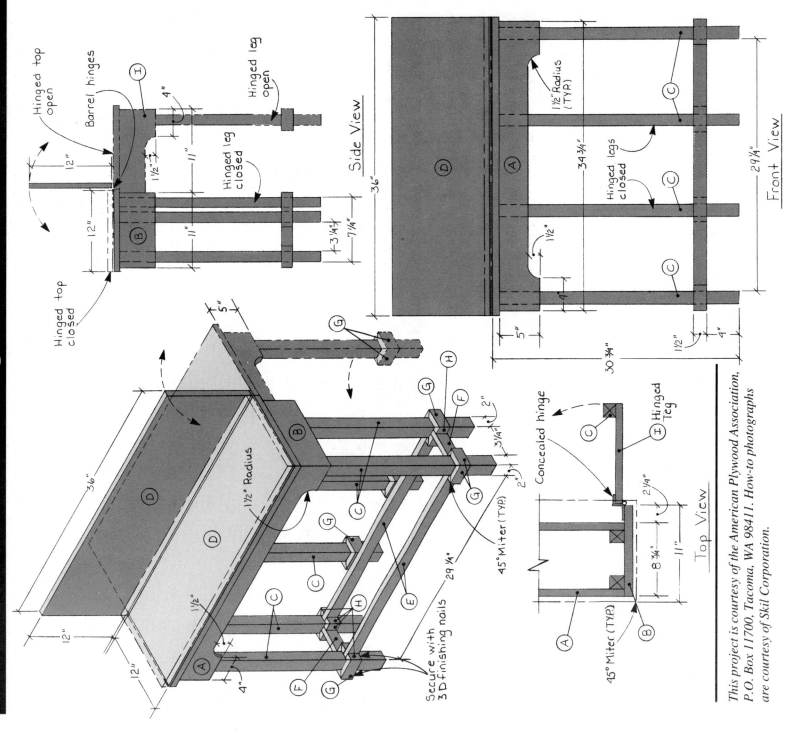

Hinged top open

Barrel hinges

Hinged leg open

Hinged top closed

Hinged leg closed

(H)

4"

1½"

11"

12"

12"

(B)

11"

7¼"

3¾"

Side View

Hinged top closed

36"

1½" Radius (TYP)

(C)

(D)

(A)

34¾"

Hinged legs closed

(C)

(C)

1½"

4"

Front View

29¼"

5"

30¾"

1½"

4"

(G)

5"

2"

3¾"

2"

(H)

(F)

(G)

(D)

(D)

1½" Radius

36"

(B)

(C)

(G)

(C)

(E)

45° Miter (TYP)

29¼"

(H)

(C)

12"

(A)

1½"

12"

4"

(F)

(G)

(G)

Secure with 3D finishing nails

Concealed hinge

(C)

(H) Hinged leg

2¼"

8¾"

11"

(A)

(B)

45° Miter (TYP)

Top View

This project is courtesy of the American Plywood Association, P.O. Box 11700, Tacoma, WA 98411. How-to photographs are courtesy of Skil Corporation.

Cutting List

A	Apron	3/4 x 5 x 34 3/4	1
B	Side	3/4 x 5 x 11	2
C	Leg	2 x 2 x 30 maple	6
D	Top	3/4 x 12 x 36	2
E	Long rail	3/4 x 1 1/2 x 29 1/4	2
F	Short rail	3/4 x 1 1/2 x 3 1/4	2
G	Leg trim	3/4 x 1 1/2 x 3 1/2	16
H	Leg trim	3/4 x 1 3/8 x 1 1/2	16
I	Hinged apron	3/4 x 5 x 11	2

Note: All material is plywood unless otherwise indicated. All dimensions are in inches.

nails to secure the legs. Also, use a carpenter's square to ensure that the legs are perpendicular to the hinged apron.

Remeasure the distance for the long rail (E) and the short rail (F), then custom cut the four rails to fit. Also, custom cut all of the leg trim (G, H) and secure with carpenter's glue and 3d finishing nails. You will have to predrill the holes in the narrower leg trim pieces (H). If you do not, the wood may split.

Now, attach each of the hinged apron assemblies to the main unit using hinges. The hinges must be attached to the inside edge of the hinged apron as well as to the inside edge of the side workpiece (B). Use two hinges for each hinged apron assembly. Complete the project by attaching the remaining top to the table assembly with four barrel hinges.

FINISHING. Remove all of the hinges and finish sand the entire project, making sure that you dull the plywood edges. Sink all nailheads and fill in any blemishes with a good wood filler.

Remove the fine dust particles with a damp cloth and then apply an antique finish, following the manufacturer's directions for application.

❖

Figure 1.

If you do not have a drum sander, use sandpaper wrapped around a dowel to sand the apron contours. The larger the diameter of the dowel, the easier it is to sand. Sand with the contour and not into the edge. Sanding into the edge can result in wood splitting.

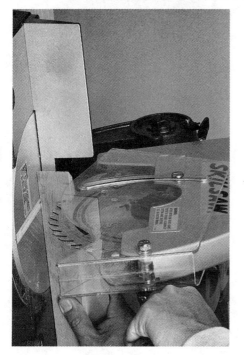

Figure 2.

A power miter box is the ideal tool for cutting the leg trim (G, H). The shorter leg trim (H) must be cut from a longer length of material.

Apothecary Chest

This handsome pine chest will add country flavor to your room's decor.

his nostalgic chest is reminiscent of those found in nearly every neighborhood drugstore years ago. Our version of the apothecary chest is designed to be used as a nightstand in your bedroom or as an end table in your living room or family room. Though it appears to have 12 drawers, there are actually only six drawers, each with a false divider. Grooves cut into each drawer front and 12 knobs give the chest its authentic appearance.

SKILL LEVEL. This project is well suited to intermediate-level and advanced woodworkers.

TIPS. If you have difficulty making accurate dado joints, substitute with doweling or with wood biscuits. Of course, you will then have to recalculate the dimensions for such workpieces as the shelves (D). Finding material that is 1 in. in size requires special milling. You can do this yourself using a thickness planer, or you can have the milling done at your local lumberyard or lumber supply store.

CONSTRUCTION. It is going to be difficult to find 1 in. material of the appropriate width to form the wider workpieces. Therefore, you will have to joint the edges with a portable planer before edge-gluing. Make sure there are no gaps in the edges to be joined and use only light clamping pressure.

Cut the sides (A), top (B), shelves (D), top/bottom shelves (E) and dividers (I) to their appropriate lengths; however, make them approximately ⅛ in. wider than is called for in the cutting list. Follow this up by jointing the edges to their appropriate widths.

Install a dado blade in your table saw and cut the dado and rabbet joints into both of the side workpieces (A). Afterward, smooth out the dado with a wide wood chisel. Make sure that you do not sand the workpieces that will fit into the dado. This will result in unsightly gaps that will have to be filled in, which may lead to loose joints.

Now, reset your dado blade and cut full-length rabbets into the two side workpieces as well as into the top/bottom shelves (E). These rabbets will accommodate the plywood back (C).

Dry-assemble the shelves, dividers and sides to one another, making sure that everything fits properly. Be especially careful to locate the center dividers properly.

Disassemble the unit, and then use a biscuit joiner to locate the center dividers to the adjacent workpieces. Biscuit joiners create a very strong bond and allow you to make quick, accurate cuts.

Apothecary Chest

Figure 1.

Use a biscuit joiner to attach the dividers (I) to the shelves (D) and the top/bottom workpieces (E).

Attach the dividers to the shelves with carpenter's glue and biscuit wafers. Then attach the two side workpieces with carpenter's glue and square the assembly. Use bar clamps to apply light clamping pressure. Allow the glue to dry overnight before removing the clamps.

Once the glue has dried, remove the bar clamps from the assembled project. Custom cut and install the plywood back (C) with carpenter's glue and brads.

Now, custom cut the base assembly. This consists of the base sides (H), base front (G), base top (F) and base back (O). Take your time when mitering the edges of the base sides and the base front. Use a power miter box to ensure accuracy.

Assemble the base workpieces to one another with carpenter's glue and 4d finishing nails. Sink all nailheads. Then cut the cleats (P, Q) and install with carpenter's glue and 1 in. brads. The cleats help support the base top (F).

Install a rounding over bit in your router and rout the showing edges of the base top (F) as well as the chest top (B).

Figure 2.

A power miter box makes excellent mitered edges for joining the base front (G) to the base side (H).

Attach the base assembly to the chest assembly using carpenter's glue and 4d finishing nails. Drive the nails in from underneath the base top.

Secure the top (B) to the chest assembly with carpenter's glue. For a stronger joint, drive 1½ in. flathead wood screws from underneath the base top (F). Predrill these holes and countersink the screw heads.

Measure the drawer cavities to ensure that the drawers will fit as designed. Then cut all of the drawer faces (J), drawer fronts (K), drawer backs (L) and drawer sides (M) to size. Mill rabbets into the drawer sides with a dado blade installed in your table saw. Clean out the cuts with a sharp wood chisel. Follow this up by cutting grooves along the inside bottom edge of all of the drawer sides, backs and fronts. Dry-assemble these workpieces and then custom cut the drawer bottoms (N) to fit. Remember that the drawer bottoms should be approximately ⅛ in.

How-to photographs are courtesy of Skil Corporation.

Figure 3.
Using a rounding over bit, rout the rounding edges of the base assembly before attaching the base assembly to the apothecary unit.

shorter in length and in width so that it *floats*. Note that if the drawer bottoms were glued in place, variances in humidity could easily result in the joints becoming loose or in some of the workpieces cracking. When you are satisfied with the result, assemble all of the drawer parts to one another — with the exception of the drawer faces (J) — with carpenter's glue. Double-check for squareness.

Each drawer face (J) has two slits in it that makes it look as if it is actually two drawers. To create the cut, install a regular saw blade in your table saw and make the perpendicular cuts with the aid of a miter gauge. Drill holes for the knobs. You will have to counterbore a larger hole to accommodate the knob screw that fits inside the back of each drawer face. Accomplish this by using a 1 in. diameter Forstner bit installed in your drill press. Then attach the drawer faces to the drawer fronts with No. 8 by 1¼ in. flathead wood screws driven inside the drawer unit. Only two screws are needed to secure each drawer face to its mating drawer front. Do not glue this joint, because that would make knob replacement impossible.

Cutting List

A	Side	1 x 11¼ x 20½	2
B	Top	1 x 12¼ x 29¾	1
C	Back	¼ x 19½ x 26¾ plywood	1
D	Shelf	1 x 11 x 26¾	2
E	Top/bottom shelf	1 x 11¼ x 26¾	2
F	Base top	¾ x 11¼ x 27¾	2
G	Base front	¾ x 3 x 29¼	1
H	Base side	¾ x 3 x 12	2
I	Divider	1 x 5½ x 11	3
J	Drawer face	1 x 5⅜ x 12⅛	6
K	Drawer front	¾ x 5⅜ x 10⅝	6
L	Drawer back	¾ x 5⅜ x 11⅜	6
M	Drawer side	¾ x 5⅜ x 9¾	12
N	Drawer bottom	¼ x 9 x 11½ plywood	6
O	Base back	¾ x 2¼ x 27¾ plywood	1
P	Front/back cleat	¾ x ¾ x 10	4
Q	Side cleat	¾ x ¾ x 8	2

Note: All material is pine unless otherwise indicated. All dimensions are in inches.

FINISHING. Remove the drawer knobs and fill in any blemishes with a nontoxic wood filler. Then finish sand the entire project.

Decide on the kind of finish that you wish to apply, such as a stain or antique finish. Be sure to follow the manufacturer's instructions for application.

❖

Apothecary Chest

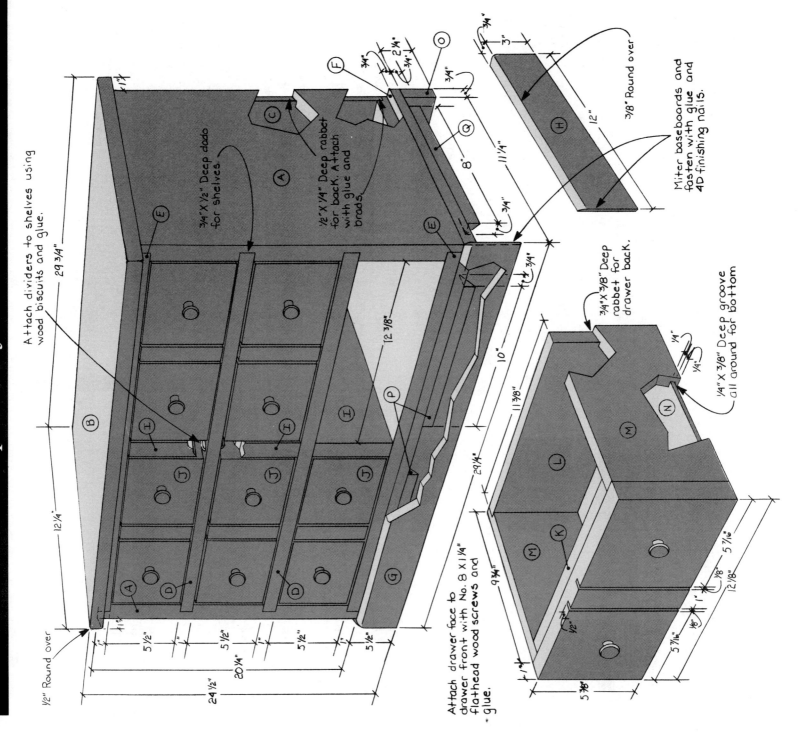

Attach dividers to shelves using wood biscuits and glue.

3/4" x 1/2" Deep dado for shelves.

1/2" x 1/4" Deep rabbet for back. Attach with glue and brads.

1/2" Round over

Attach drawer face to drawer front with No. 8 x 1 1/4" flathead wood screws and glue.

Miter baseboards and fasten with glue and 4D finishing nails.

3/8" Round over

3/4" x 3/8" Deep rabbet for drawer back.

1/4" x 3/8" Deep groove all around for bottom

29 3/4"

12 1/4"

24 1/2"

20 1/4"

5 1/2"   5 1/2"   5 1/2"

1"   1"   1"   1"

12 3/8"

11 1/4"

8"

3/4"   3/4"

10"

3"   3/4"

12"

11 3/8"

29 1/4"

9 3/4"

5 7/16"   5 7/16"

12 1/8"

5 7/8"

1"   1/8"   1/2"   1/8"

1/4"   1/4"

A B C D E F G H I J K L M N O P Q

73

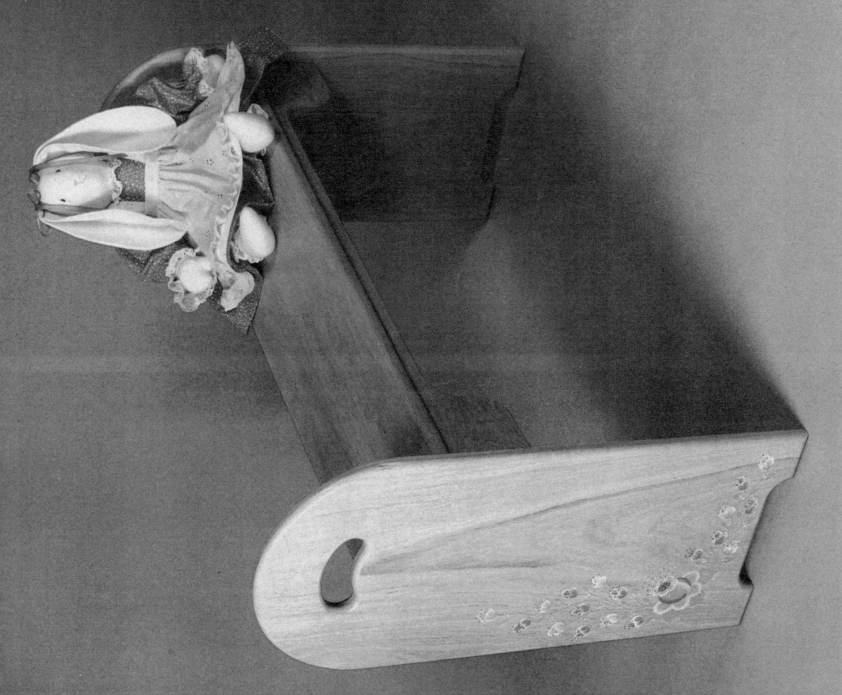

Colonial Bench

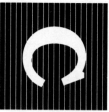

onstructed of oak, this sturdy bench has a Colonial look, with its rounded sides and contoured rails. Its simplicity is part of its charm, but it is easily dressed up. Tole painting adds a country look and is just one way to personalize the bench. Stencils, rosemaling or appliqués are other ways to customize your bench to make it a charming accent for just about any room, from rec rooms to bedrooms.

SKILL LEVEL. This attractive but simple bench is ideal for beginning to intermediate-level woodworkers. It calls for stopped dadoes cut into both side workpieces (A) to accommodate the seat (B).

TIPS. A saber saw, a router and a table saw are the primary power tools you will need to construct this project. Of course, you will also need to drill holes and sand inside the hand pulls, both of which can be accomplished with power tools.

If you do not have a table saw to cut the stopped dadoes in the side workpieces (A), use a router equipped with a 3/4 in. straight bit.

CONSTRUCTION. Carefully lay out all of the project parts using a straight rule and a bar compass or a circle template. If your material is not to the

---

A handsome bench for your foyer doubles as a handy place to sit when putting on your boots or tying your toddler's shoelaces!

---

widths specified, you may have to edge-glue several narrower pieces first. If so, make sure that you do a good job of jointing the two edges to be edge-glued using a power plane or a stationary jointer. Check the seams before doing the actual gluing. There should be no gaps at this stage. Then apply a good carpenter's glue (yellow glue) and use bar clamps to tighten the joint. A common mistake is to clamp too tightly. A good safeguard to prevent overtightening is to use one hand, not two, to tighten. Even when using this procedure, do not bear down on the clamp.

The best method for cutting the workpieces is by ripping them slightly oversize on your table saw and dressing the edges with a jointer to achieve the final size. Then crosscut each workpiece to its precise length on your table saw.

Cut out the design in both rails (C) and the two sides (A) with a band saw or saber saw. Make sure that you use a fine-tooth blade to avoid splintering the wood. Follow this up by sanding the edges with an abrasive sander or a drum sander. All of the edges must be smooth for the routing process.

Drill two holes for the handhold in each of the side workpieces. Use a backup board when drilling. A Forstner bit is an ideal drill accessory to use for

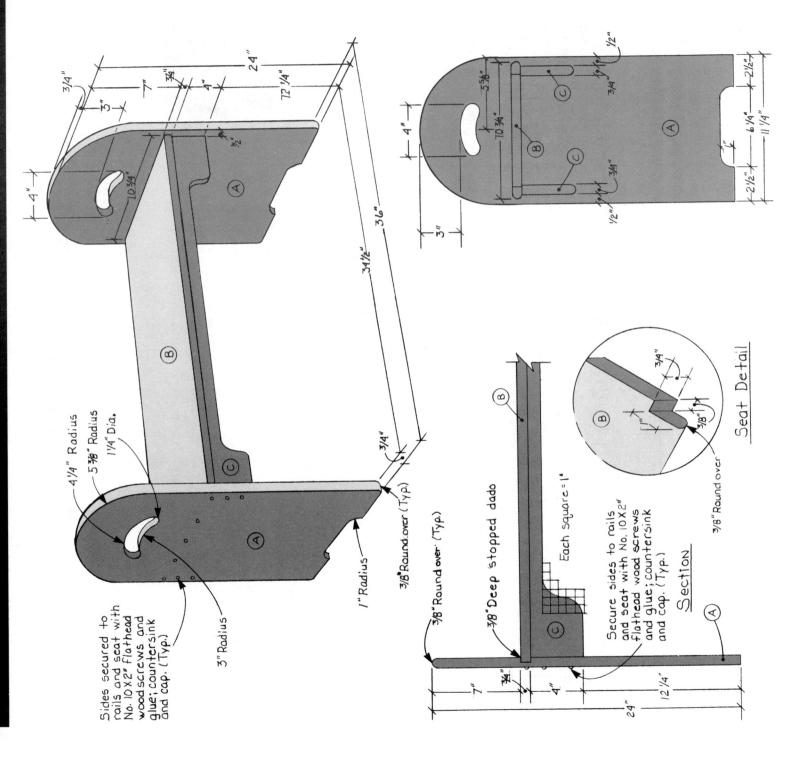

Colonial Bench

3/4"
3"
7"
3/4"
4"
24"
1/2"
4"
10 3/4"
12 1/4"
36"
34 1/2"

A

B

C

1/2"
5 5/8"
4"
10 3/4"
3/4"
3/4"
3"
3/4"
2 1/2"
6 1/4"
11 1/4"
2 1/2"
1"

A

B

C

4 1/4" Radius
5 3/8" Radius
1 1/4" Dia.

Sides secured to
rails and seat with
No. 10x2" Flathead
wood screws and
glue; countersink
and cap. (Typ.)

3" Radius

1" Radius

3/8" Round over (Typ.)

3/4"

A

B

C

3/8" Round over (Typ.)

3/8" Deep stopped dado

Each square = 1"

Secure sides to rails
and seat with No. 10x2"
flathead wood screws
and glue; countersink
and cap. (Typ.)

7"
3/4"
4"
24"

Section

3/4"

1"

3/8"

3/8" Round over

B

Seat Detail

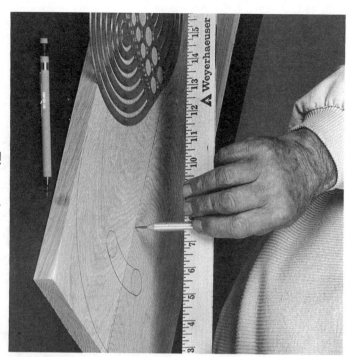

Figure 1.

Lay out the handhold and the perimeter of the side work-piece (A) with a straightedge, bar compass and circle template. A circle template can be purchased from an art supply store.

obtaining smooth, precisely cut holes. Then complete the handhold by cutting out the waste area with a saber saw. Work slowly to avoid inaccurate cutting.

Finish sand the insides of both handholds and both side workpieces. A small drum sander is ideal for this type of sanding.

Create the stopped dadoes in the side workpieces using a table saw equipped with a dado blade. Set the blade, then make a 3/4 in. wide and 3/8 in. deep cut. It is imperative that you test the dado blade by cutting scrap material first to ensure that the blade is cutting at the appropriate width and depth and also to mark the location points where the dado is to begin and end. After you are satisfied with the results, make your

How-to photographs are courtesy of Skil Corporation.

Cutting List

A	Side	3/4 x 11 1/4 x 24	2
B	Seat	3/4 x 10 3/4 x 35 1/4	1
C	Rail	3/4 x 4 x 34 1/2	2

Note: All material is oak unless otherwise indicated. All dimensions are in inches.

Figure 2.

Here we are forming the stopped dadoes in the side workpieces (A). As an alternative to using a table saw equipped with a dado blade, we are using a router equipped with a straight bit. The router is guided along a clamped straightedge. Note that the locations for the beginning and the end of the cut are marked on the workpiece. If you have never dadoed using a router, you need to first practice on a piece of scrap material. You need to work slowly, as the router will get away from you if you are not careful. Also, make progressively deeper cuts. Do not go to the full depth of the dado.

Colonial Bench

dado cut. Use a sharp wood chisel to clean out the dado cuts.

Notch the ends of the seat (B) so that the pins that remain will fit into the dadoes that you cut out into the side workpieces. Use a saber saw or a band saw, and make sure that the joint fits snugly.

Next, equip your router with a ⅜ in. rounding over bit, with pilot installed. Carefully rout the sides (A), the seat (B) and the rails (C) in the locations specified in the illustration. Make sure that you move the router counterclockwise around the workpiece and that the workpiece is held securely to the workbench while routing.

ASSEMBLY. Dry-assemble the workpieces to ensure that all of the joints are tight. Then use

Figure 3.

Notice how the ends of the seat (B) fit into the seat's stopped dado. The seat, therefore, must be notched with a band saw or a saber saw to the shape shown.

TOLE PAINTING

Figure 5.

Apply paint, one color at a time, to the transferred design.

Figure 4.

Transfer the design pattern you have drawn onto the project workpiece. Use graphite paper to transfer the pattern.

Here is a close-up of the painted design.

carpenter's glue to assemble the unit. Use a combination of bar clamps and C-clamps to hold the unit together. Place the bench on a flat surface to make sure that it is square. Once the glue has dried, predrill screw holes and secure the assembly with No. 10 by 2 in. flathead wood screws. Counterbore the holes and then cover with wood plugs.

FINISHING. Give the entire project a thorough sanding. Be sure to remove all dust particles from the project before finishing.

Apply a stencil pattern or a rosemaling design to the sides. When the application is dry, apply a wood stain or a sealer. Carefully follow the manufacturer's

Figure 6.

Assemble the bench using glue; do not secure with wood screws at this time. Make sure that the unit is standing on a flat surface before clamping. Once the glue has dried, predrill the fastener holes and install the screws.

instructions for application. If you use stain, you will probably have to remove any excess stain with a clean cloth, wiping with the grain. After you have applied the stain, allow it to dry.

Give the project an application of a good clear sealer. When this coat is dry, give it a light sanding.

Complete the project by applying a coat of a satin polyurethane finish.

❖ ──────── ❖

Hobby Center

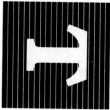

his wall unit is a dream come true, with its many shelves, drawers and cabinet spaces. It is the ultimate organizer, and now you can build it at an affordable price. Perfect for a bedroom, living room, family room or den, this project will test your woodworking skills while paying off in big dividends. It also can be modified to suit your particular needs.

SKILL LEVEL. This is a project suitable for intermediate-level to advanced woodworkers.

TIPS. Instead of cutting in grooves for shelf standards, you can make the shelves fixed, as we did. Notice that all of the doors have raised panels. For detailed step-by-step photos on how to make raised door panels, refer to the Dry Sink project.

CONSTRUCTION.

Begin by constructing the lower carcass first, then progress to the upper shelving unit. Cut out the workpieces for the lower carcass, which consist of the lower sides (ZZ), bottom inner sides (D), bottom inner dividers (C), right bottom (X), cabinet shelf (Y) and cabinet top (V). Dado the workpieces that will accommodate the plywood back (U). Dado the bottom inner dividers (C) to accommodate the shelf (Y).

Secure the carcass with carpenter's glue and 4d finishing nails. Sink all nailheads and fill in the re-

cesses with a nontoxic wood filler. Make sure that the assembly is square. Attach all of the cabinet frames, which include workpieces Z and AA through II. Secure these with carpenter's glue and 4d finishing nails. Make sure that you miter the edges where parts HH and II join one another. Also, dowel parts BB and CC to the adjacent faces.

Now, cut dadoes into the cabinet top (V) to accommodate the upper shelving units. Use a router equipped with a straight bit. Also, use a straightedge to ensure a nice, straight cut.

Next, cut the sides (B), shelf walls (E) and left shelf divider (F) to their appropriate lengths. Dado these workpieces to accommodate the shelves, and then custom cut the shelves to fit. Also, rout a rabbet into the inside edges of the shelf walls (E) so that the

center panel (K) will fit in place. Rabbet the back edges of the appropriate workpieces to accommodate the plywood back (U).

Now, assemble the entire upper unit using carpenter's glue and 4d finishing nails. Custom cut the remaining workpieces to suit the assem-

bly that you have just completed. Then attach this upper unit to the cabinet carcass with carpenter's glue. Install the central panel, and then custom cut all of the cabinet frames to suit the assembly. Again, attach the cabinet frame with glue and 4d finishing nails.

With a hobby center like this one, you may just become organized!

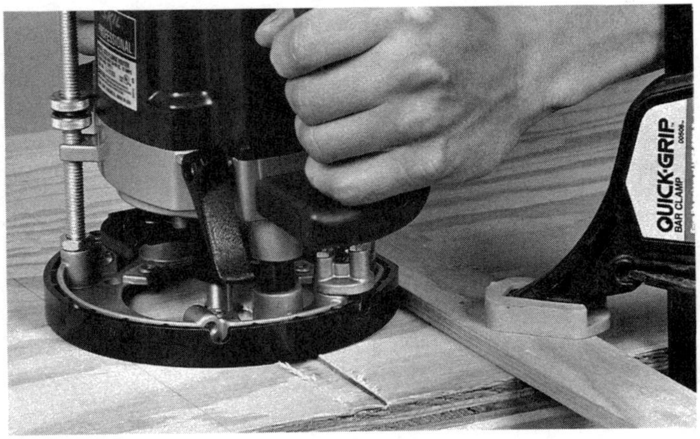

Figure 1.
Use a router equipped with a straight bit to dado the side workpieces (B). Use a straightedge to guarantee a straight cut. Make progressively deeper passes to minimize wood splintering and wood burning.

Custom cut the crown molding (of your choice) with a power miter box and attach to the unit.

Custom make all of the drawers to fit the assembled unit. Rout decorative edges into all of the drawer

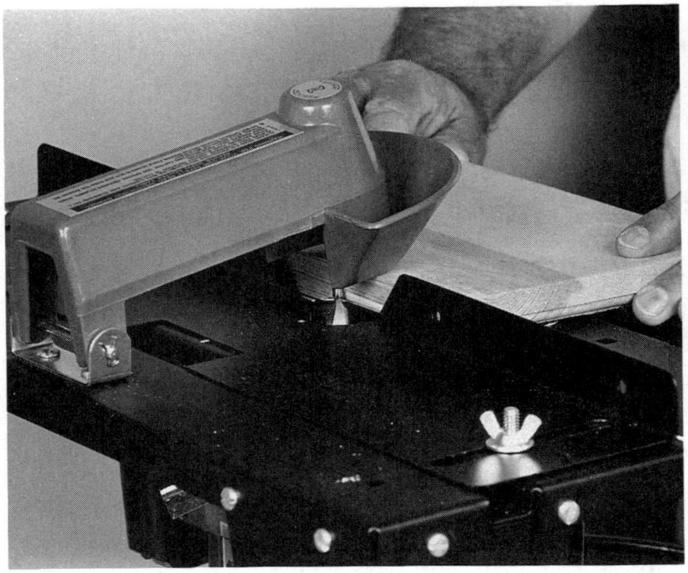

Figure 2.
Install a decorative bit in your router table and rout the edges of the medium drawer faces (NN).

Cutting List

A	Top	3/4 x 16 3/4 x 89 1/2	1
B	Side	3/4 x 23 1/4 x 70	2
C	Bottom inner divider	3/4 x 22 3/4 x 29 1/2	2
D	Bottom inner side	3/4 x 23 x 29 3/4	2
E	Shelf wall	3/4 x 16 1/4 x 66 1/4	2
F	Left shelf divider	3/4 x 16 1/4 x 43	1
G	Right shelf divider	3/4 x 16 1/4 x 22	1
H	Shelf	3/4 x 17 9/16 x 16 1/4	2
I	Shelf	3/4 x 17 3/16 x 16 1/4	2
J	Shelf	3/4 x 33 7/8 x 16 1/4	4
K	Center panel	1/2 x 18 1/2 x 65 1/2	1
L	Outer shelf frame	3/4 x 1 1/2 x 70 pine	2
M	Center shelf frame	3/4 x 1 1/2 x 64 1/2 pine	2
N	Upper shelf frame	3/4 x 5 1/2 x 87 pine	1
O	Shelf frame	3/4 x 1 1/2 x 33 3/8 pine	2
P	Shelf frame	3/4 x 1 1/2 x 41 1/4 pine	1
Q	Shelf frame	3/4 x 1 1/2 x 21 3/4 pine	1

faces (JJ, NN, QQ). At this time, also make all of the doors with raised panels.

Drill holes for all of the hardware and hinge all of the doors. Also, install magnetic door latches.

This project is courtesy of Georgia-Pacific Corporation, 133 Peachtree St. N.E., P.O. Box 105605, Atlanta, GA 30348. How-to photographs are courtesy of Skil Corporation.

Code	Part	Dimensions	Qty
R	Shelf frame	3/4 x 1 1/2 x 17 1/4 pine	2
S	Top front molding	4 x 96 crown molding	1
T	Top side molding	4 x 24 crown molding	2
U	Back	1/2 x 89 x 95	1
V	Cabinet top	3/4 x 24 1/2 x 89 1/2	1
W	Left bottom	3/4 x 13 1/2 x 23 1/4	1
X	Right bottom	3/4 x 55 1/2 x 23 1/4	1
Y	Cabinet shelf	3/4 x 22 1/2 x 22 3/4	1
Z	Cabinet frame	3/4 x 2 1/2 x 29 1/4 pine	4
AA	Cabinet frame	3/4 x 2 1/2 x 25 1/4 pine	2
BB	Cabinet frame	3/4 x 1 1/2 x 9 pine	4
CC	Cabinet frame	3/4 x 2 1/2 x 9 pine	1
DD	Cabinet frame	3/4 x 1 1/2 x 20 pine	1
EE	Cabinet frame	3/4 x 1 1/2 x 51 pine	1
FF	Cabinet frame	3/4 x 2 1/2 x 51 pine	1
GG	Cabinet frame	3/4 x 1 1/2 x 13 pine	1
HH	Cabinet top trim	3/4 x 1 1/2 x 93 pine	1
II	Cabinet top trim	3/4 x 1 1/2 x 25 3/4 pine	2
JJ	Small drawer face	3/4 x 4 1/2 x 10 pine	1
KK	Small drawer front/back	1/2 x 3 3/8 x 8	2
LL	Small drawer side	1/2 x 3 3/8 x 15 1/2	2
MM	Small drawer bottom	1/4 x 7 1/2 x 15 1/2	4
NN	Medium drawer bottom	1/4 x 6 3/4 x 10 pine	3
OO	Medium drawer front/back	3/4 x 5 5/8 x 8	6
PP	Medium drawer side	1/2 x 5 5/8 x 15 1/2	6
QQ	Large drawer face	3/4 x 12 7/8 x 14 pine	2
RR	Large drawer front/back	1/2 x 11 3/4 x 12	4
SS	Large drawer side	1/2 x 11 3/4 x 15 1/2	4
TT	Large drawer bottom	1/4 x 11 1/2 x 15 1/2	2
UU	Cabinet stile	3/4 x 1 1/2 x 26 1/4 pine	6
VV	Left cabinet rail	3/4 x 1 1/2 x 10 pine	2
WW	Paired cabinet rail	3/4 x 1 1/2 x 11 pine	4
XX	Left panel	1/2 x 9 3/4 x 24 pine	1
YY	Paired panel	1/2 x 9 1/4 x 24 pine	1
ZZ	Lower side	3/4 x 23 1/4 x 29 1/4	2

Note: All material is plywood unless otherwise indicated. All dimensions are in inches.

FINISHING. Remove all of the hardware. Then sink all nailheads and fill in all recesses and blemishes with a good nontoxic wood filler. Finish sand the entire project, making sure that you dull all sharp wood edges.

Use a shop vacuum to remove all fine dust particles, and then apply a coat of paint sealer. Follow this up by sanding lightly with a pad sander, and then apply your choice of paint. Another paint application may be required, depending on the type of paint that you use. Reinstall the doorknobs and attach the drawer faces to the drawers with several drywall screws driven from inside the drawer. Also, reinstall the door hinges, along with the magnetic door latches.

Hobby Center

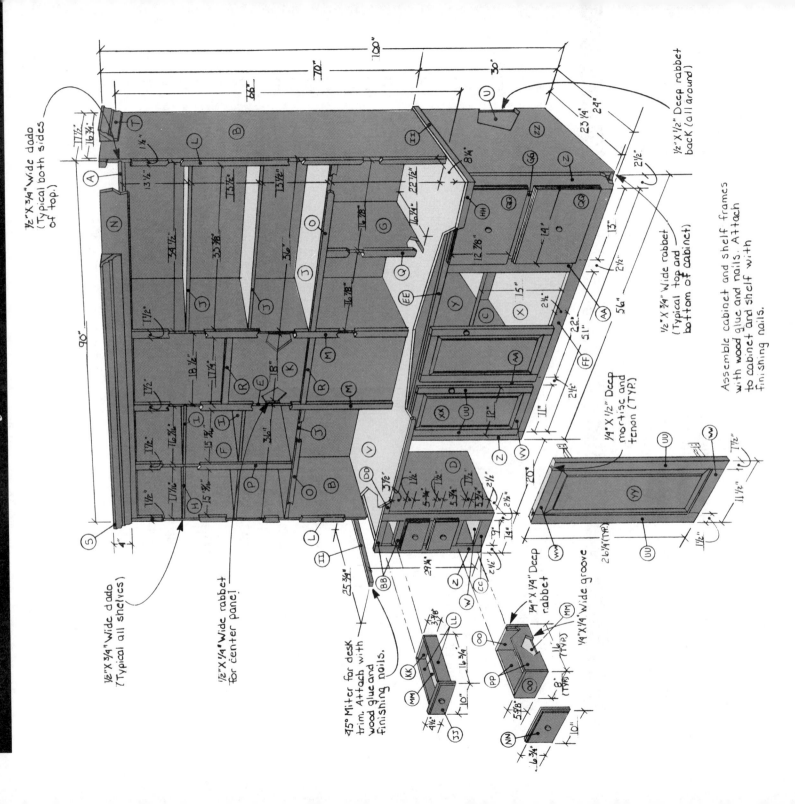

½" X ¾" wide dado (Typical both sides of top.)

½" X ¾" wide dado (Typical all shelves)

½" X ¼" wide rabbet for center panel

45° Miter for desk trim. Attach with wood glue and finishing nails.

½" X ½" Deep rabbet back (all around)

½" X ¾" wide rabbet (Typical top and bottom of cabinet)

Assemble cabinet and shelf frames with wood glue and nails. Attach to cabinet and shelf with finishing nails.

¼" X ½" Deep mortise and tenon (TYP.)

¼" X ¼" Deep rabbet

¼" X ¼" wide groove

84

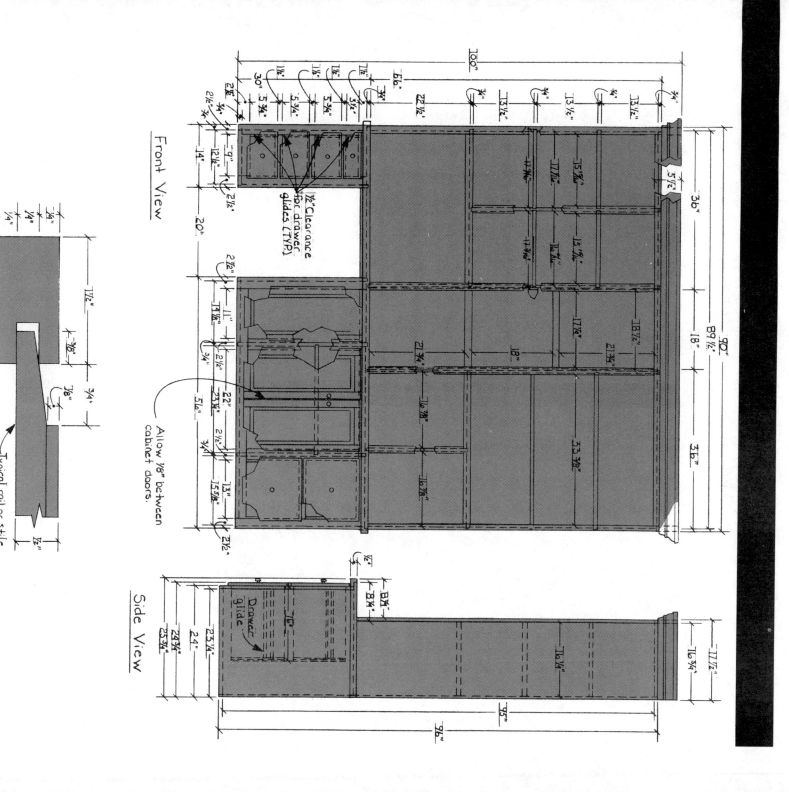

Front View

Side View

Door Detail

Typical rail or stile

½" Clearance for drawer glides (TYP.)

Allow ⅛" between cabinet doors.

Drawer glide

85

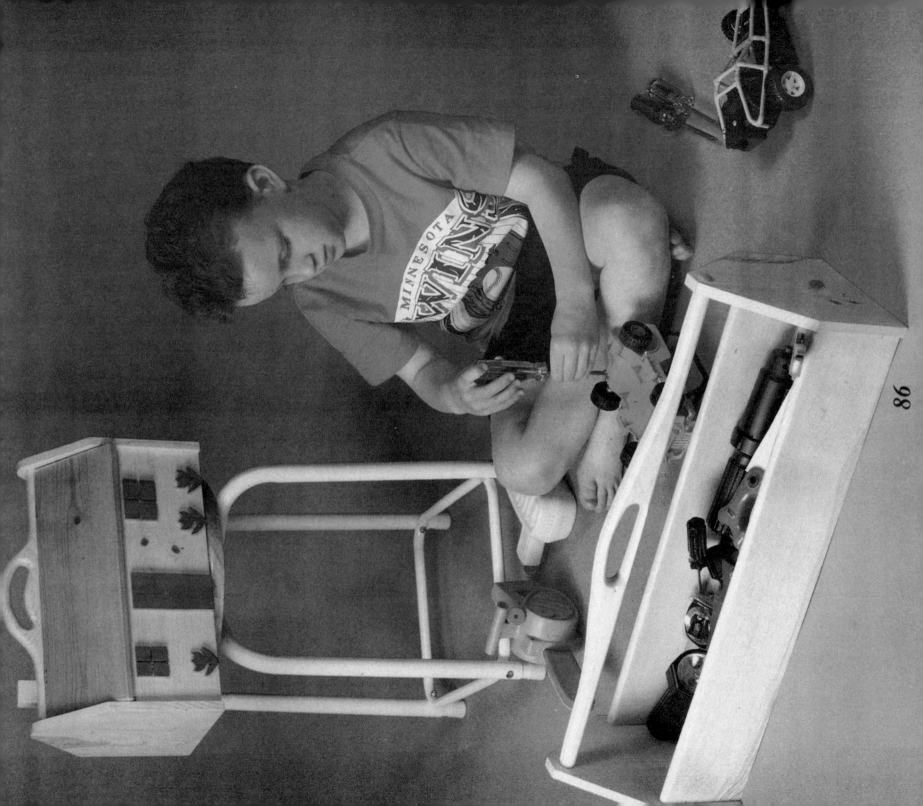

Two Children's Toolboxes

Almost every boy and girl loves to play with toy hammers, screwdrivers and pliers. Here are toolboxes that can be used for those pretend toys or for the real thing. Building these toolboxes is also a great way to introduce youngsters to the art of working with wood. By following good safety rules and with the aid of Mom or Dad, youngsters will enjoy helping to build these projects. While we have fancied up only the girl's toolbox, you could do the same thing for the boy's version, using cutouts of tools, or dinosaurs or cars.

SKILL LEVEL. These two toolboxes are good projects for young beginning woodworkers. Most of us acquired our interest in woodworking at a young age, and these two toolboxes are an inviting way to get your children interested in woodworking.

TIPS. If you are going to have children participate in the construction of the project, you need to establish beforehand just what you want them to do for the project and what you don't want them to do. If the child is very young — under ten years old, for example — you certainly will want to make it clear that power tools are off limits. However, you can have the youngster hammer some of the nails after you predrill the nail holes.

Do you know a budding woodworker who needs a toolbox? If so, we've got just the project for you.

Begin by explaining to the child how the project will be constructed, the types of tools that will be used and who will do what. The more information you give, the more interest you will generate in the child. Tell the youngster the name of each of the tools and accessories and how each will be used to accomplish certain tasks.

GIRL'S TOOLBOX CONSTRUCTION. Using a combination square, lay out all of the parts to be cut on the appropriate material. Draw the handle contour on the handle workpiece (D), and trace tulip patterns onto longer lengths of 1/4 in. plywood to form the tulips (J). Note that we used scrap cherry plywood. Also, lay out one of the side workpieces (A).

Cut the bottom (C), one of the sides (A) and the chimney (F) to shape using a scroll saw. When finished, use the side workpiece (A) to trace the other side workpiece. Then cut this workpiece to shape.

Cut the three edges, but not the beveled areas, of the front/back (B) and the roof (E) workpieces on a scroll saw. Then tilt the scroll saw bed to 45 degrees and cut the bevels required in these workpieces.

Carefully lay out the handle section of the handle workpiece (D) using French curves and a circle template. Cut out the outside contour with a scroll saw,

Two Children's Toolboxes

and then drill a hole in the handhold area and cut this out on your scroll saw.

Use a stationary disk sander to sand and square all of the cut edges in the workpieces that you have cut thus far. Then use an abrasive sander to sand the outside edge of the handle contour. Similarly, use the stationary disk sander to smooth the bevels in the front/back and the roof.

Sand the inside edges of the handhold by wrapping a piece of sandpaper around a dowel. Make sure that the workpiece is held in a vise while sanding. Round over the showing edges of the handle with a drum attachment installed in your Moto-Tool.

Cut the bevel in the chimney (F) and finish sand on a stationary disk sander.

Carefully cut the windows (G, H), door (I) and tulips (J) on your scroll saw. Work from longer lengths of material and use a wider blade when making each cut. When you are finished, lightly sand the edges and surfaces with fine grit sandpaper.

GIRL'S TOOLBOX ASSEMBLY AND FINISHING. Assemble the toolbox with 3d finishing

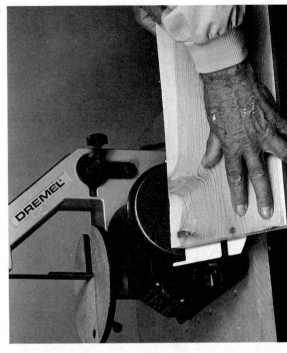

Figure 3.

Smooth the beveled edges of the roof (E) on a stationary disk sander. Work in long, smooth strokes.

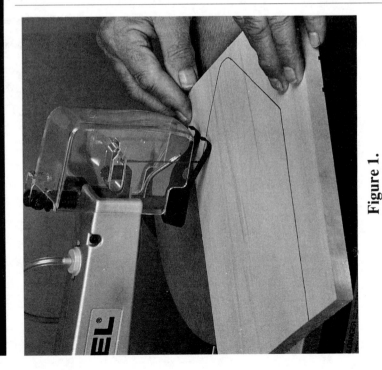

Figure 1.

Lay out the sides (A) and cut them out on a stationary scroll saw.

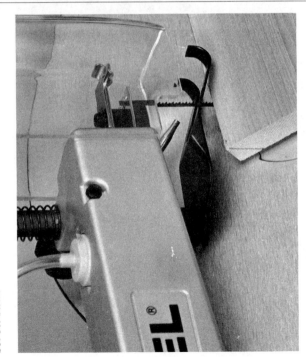

Figure 2.

Cut the bevels in the roof workpieces (E), tilting the bed of the scroll saw to 45 degrees.

Cutting List

GIRL'S TOOLBOX

A	Side		1/2 x 7 x 10	2
B	Front/back		1/2 x 6⅝ x 14	2
C	Bottom		1/2 x 5½ x 14	1
D	Handle		3/4 x 3 x 14	1
E	Roof		1/2 x 5⅜ x 14	2
F	Chimney		3/4 x 1¼ x 2¼	1
G	Large window		1/4 x 1 1/16 x 13/16	1
H	Small window	plywood	1/4 x 11/16 x 11/16	4
I	Door	plywood	1/4 x 2 x 4¼	1
J	Tulip	plywood	1/4 x 1½ x 1½	3

BOY'S TOOLBOX

AA	Side	1/2 x 7 x 8	2
BB	Front/back	1/2 x 4 x 23	2
CC	Bottom	1/2 x 5½ x 23	1
DD	Handle	3/4 x 1⅞ x 23	1

Note: All material is pine unless otherwise indicated. All dimensions are in inches.

nails and carpenter's glue. It is important that each of the nail holes be predrilled to avoid splitting the wood.

Assemble the front/back workpieces (B) to the bottom workpiece (C) with glue and finishing nails.

Next, secure the two sides to the assembled U-shaped box. At this point it is important that everything be properly aligned.

Install the handle using carpenter's glue and finishing nails. Attach the chimney (F) to one of the roof (E) workpieces. This will form the back of the roof. Now, secure the back roof and the chimney to the toolbox.

Shave off approximately 1/16 in. from the edge of the remaining roof workpiece so the roof front can be opened and closed without hitting the sides (A). Use a stationary disk sander to accomplish this.

Determine the hinge locations on the edges of the roof. It is not necessary to mortise out this area.

Place the windows (G, H), door (I) and tulips (J) onto the front of the toolbox. To do this, the toolbox needs to be laid on its back side. Position the workpieces in an appealing configuration, and then use a dab of carpenter's glue to secure each workpiece. Allow the glue to dry overnight before moving the toolbox.

Sink all nailheads and fill in the recesses with a nontoxic wood filler. When the wood filler has dried, sand smooth.

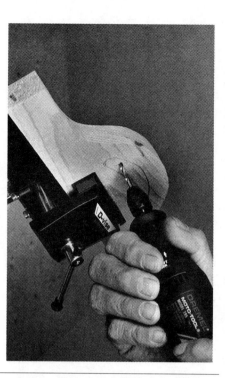

Figure 4.
Predrill a hole into the handhold area of the handle (D). Drill a starter hole for the scroll saw blade.

This project and all photography are courtesy of Dremel, 4915 21st St., Racine, WI 53406. The tools used include the 16 in. scroll saw (model 1671), shaper/router table (model 231), disc/belt sander (model 1731), Moto-Tool (model 395) and D-Vise (model 2214).

89

Two Children's Toolboxes

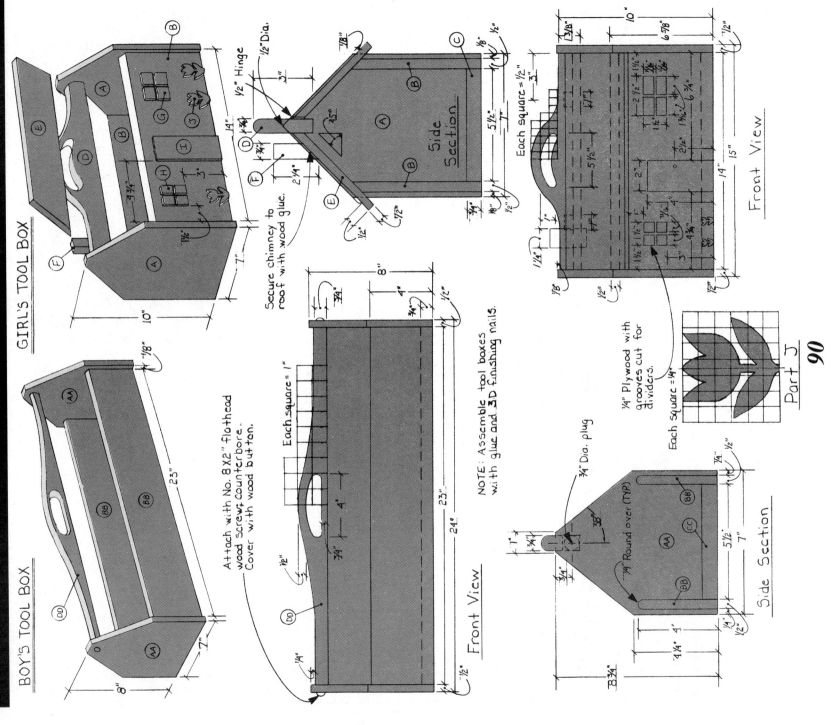

GIRL'S TOOL BOX

BOY'S TOOL BOX

Secure chimney to roof with wood glue.

½" Dia.
½" Hinge

Side Section

Front View

Each square = ½"

¼" Plywood with grooves cut for dividers.

Part J

Front View

Each square = 1"

NOTE: Assemble tool boxes with glue and 3D finishing nails.

Attach with No. 8X2" flathead wood screws counterbore. Cover with wood button.

¾" Dia. plug

Side Section

¼" Round over (TYP)

Each square = ¼"

90

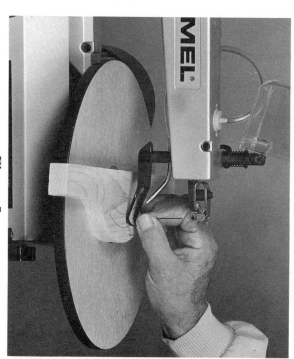

Figure 5.
Insert the scroll saw blade through the starter hole and attach the blade to the scroll saw. Then cut out the handhold.

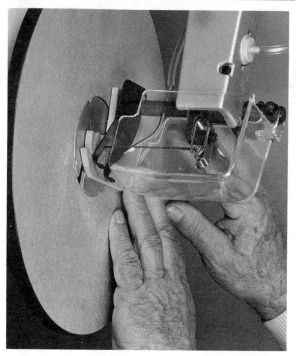

Figure 6.
Lay out the tulips (J) on a longer length of material and cut out the shapes on the scroll saw. You must have a longer length of material to avoid cutting with your fingers too close to the blade.

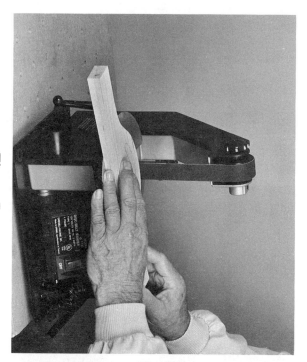

Figure 7.
Sand the outside edge of the handle (D) with an abrasive sander. It is best to work in one long, continuous light stroke.

Figure 8.
Round over the showing edges of the handle with a drum sander installed in your Moto-Tool.

Two Children's Toolboxes

Sand all of the project workpieces before spraying on a satin polyurethane finish. As an alternative you might apply tung oil.

You also can opt to paint the doors, windows and tulips various colors instead of using a contrasting wood-tone color as we did.

BOY'S TOOLBOX CONSTRUCTION. Carefully lay out each of the project parts to their overall widths and lengths on appropriately sized wood. Then lay out the handle contours with the aid of French curves, circle templates or a flexible straightedge.

Cut out each of the project parts to their appropriate size and shape on your scroll saw. When finished, use a disk sander to square the edges and an abrasive sander to sand the edges of the handle (DD). Use a drum sander installed in your Moto-Tool to help you round over the edges of the front/back (BB).

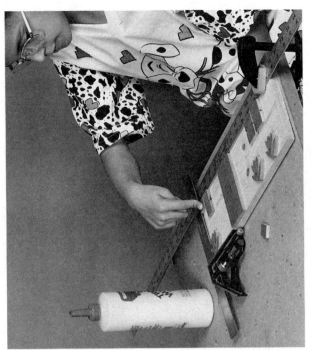

Figure 10.

Attach the windows (G, H), door (I) and tulips (J) with carpenter's glue. Use a square to help you align the unit. There is no need to clamp the small workpieces in place. Instead, apply a light dab of glue to each workpiece and then press it into place. Allow the glue to dry overnight.

92

Figure 9.

Secure the sides (A) to the bottom (C) with carpenter's glue and 3d finishing nails. Predrill each of the nail holes to avoid wood splitting. This also makes it easier for young children to drive in the nails.

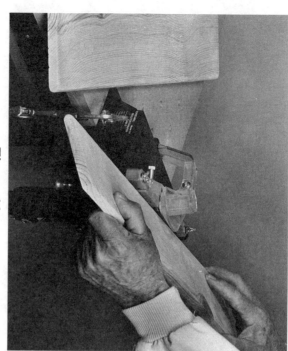

Figure 11.

Here we are rounding over the edges of the front work-piece (BB) with a drum sander installed in a Dremel router table (do not use an actual router).

Figure 12.

Secure the handle (DD) to the toolbox assembly with two flathead wood screws. These wood screw holes were counterbored and then covered with a wood button or plug.

BOY'S TOOLBOX ASSEMBLY AND FINISHING.

Finish sand all of the project parts using fine grit sandpaper.

As you did with the girl's toolbox, assemble each of the project parts with 3d finishing nails and carpenter's glue. Also, predrill each of the nail holes to avoid wood splitting.

Attach the front/back (BB) to the bottom (CC) with carpenter's glue and finishing nails. Then attach the two sides (AA) to this assembly in a similar manner. Secure the handle (DD) to the sides by first drilling for a No. 8 by 2 in. flathead wood screw. Counterbore the screw hole. Then use carpenter's glue along with finishing nails to secure the handle in place. Cover the fastener hole with a wood plug or a wood button.

Sink all nailheads and fill in the recesses with a nontoxic wood filler. When the wood filler has dried, sand smooth. Dull all showing edges.

Spray on a satin polyurethane finish. Give it at least two light coats, sanding in between dry finishes.

SAFETY FIRST. If you are working with young children, it is imperative that you pay closer attention to the safety factors. If the children are old enough to use a scroll saw, make sure that the workpiece, such as the tulip (J), is cut from a longer piece of material so that the children's fingers do not get anywhere close to the cutting blade. Also, they should wear goggles even though there may be safety shields already in place. It is also a good idea to have them wear dust masks when performing any sanding operations. This will foster good work habits and keep your little ones safe. Cover the rules of tool use and reinforce the idea of having them ask questions that will facilitate their learning and make them feel good about themselves and you.

93

❖

School Bus

Climb or ride in it, push or pull it, steer it or stash toys in it — this big yellow school bus is sure to be your toddler's favorite.

he sturdy school bus not only promises a lot of fun for kids but doubles as a convenient toy box as well. Its unique construction allows little ones to ride in the bus or push lots of toys from one room to another. It is designed to allow as many as two small children to climb aboard at once. It features a door that opens, and a simple steering mechanism that allows the driver to guide the bus.

SKILL LEVEL. This is an ideal project for the experienced woodworker who wants to try something new. It offers an opportunity to work with hardboard, and the assortment of hardware required for the steering system may be something you have never tried before. A well-equipped shop is needed to build the school bus. The unusual use of dowels and panels makes it a challenging project.

TIPS. While not a beginner's project, the school bus is easier to build than it appears. The key is measuring the base carefully before cutting. If that's done correctly, the rest falls together like a jigsaw puzzle.

CONSTRUCTION. Begin by cutting out the plywood base (A), rounding the corners and edges with a router as indicated. Drill holes and cut mortises as shown on the plan. Next, cut out the remaining plywood parts and all of the hardboard pieces, rounding the edges and corners as shown.

Drill a lift hole in the hood's top panel (M) and corner cutouts. Assemble the rear wheel covers (G, H, I) using glue and finishing nails.

Now, drill a 1 1/16 in. hole in the steering support plate (B) 1 3/16 in. from the longer side and centered on the short side. Drill holes in the dash top (C) and front (D). Round the edges of each to a 3/8 in. radius except where the parts will join when centered. Assemble with glue and finishing nails.

Drill a hole in the center of the steering wheel (E) 1/2 in. deep. Then drill holes in the door hinge cap (F).

Now, drill holes in the steel bars (FF, GG). Using a vise and a ball peen hammer, form the two steering arms and the rear axle strap. Then bend the 1/4 in. metal rod to form the steering tie rod (EE). Hammer 3/8 in. nuts into the holes in the base for the axle bolts, making sure that the nuts are flush with the surface. Place the rear axle strap in position and thread 3/8 in. bolts through the holes and into the embedded 3/8 in. nuts. Drill starter holes for four No. 8 by 3/4 in.

GROOVING THE SUPPORTS

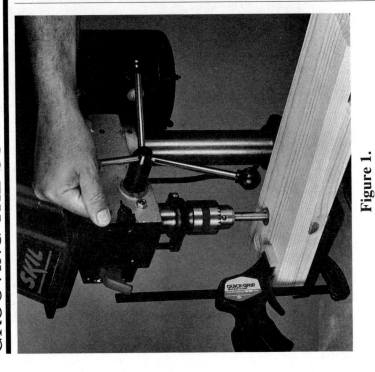

Figure 1.

Here we are making the holding jig for grooving the dowels. Drill two 1 in. diameter holes as shown.

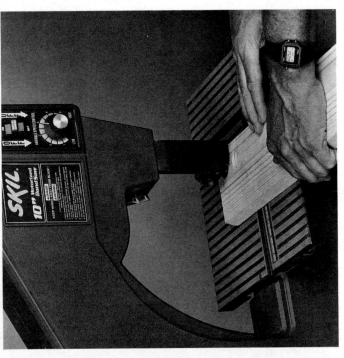

Figure 2.

Complete the dowel holding jig by ripping the wood as shown.

panhead screws. Drive in the screws and remove the bolts.

Attach the rear wheel covers (G, H, I) to the base with glue and finishing nails driven in from the bottom of the base. Glue the steering support plate (B) in place. Attach ¼ in. by 1 in. eyebolts in front of the steering support plate and then attach small pulleys to the eyebolts.

Construct the steering arm assembly as shown in the plan. Glue the steering wheel (E) to the steering column (V).

Paint all ⅛ in. hardboard panels with yellow paint and let dry. Now, cut all the dowels to length. Drill ½ in. holes into the 1 in. dowels.

Next, cut a ⅛ in. mortise ³⁄₁₆ in. deep into all of the 1 in. dowels, except those for the steering column (V). Align the mortises with the centers of the ½ in. holes previously drilled and cut the full length of each dowel.

Next, cut one mortise, ⅛ in. deep, into all of the ½ in. dowels. In two of the 11½ in. by ½ in. dowels (W), cut a second ⅛ in. mortise, ⅛ in. deep, at a 90 degree angle to the first mortise. These will form the dash supports. Set aside two 11½ in. by 1 in. dowels for the supports under the dash (U) and one 17⅞ in. by 1 in. dowel for the door hinge cap (F). Round the tops of all remaining 1 in. dowels. Sand smooth and then wax both ends of the dowels used for the door hinge (CC) and the hood hinge (AA). Check the fit of all the dowels in the base to be sure the mortises align

96

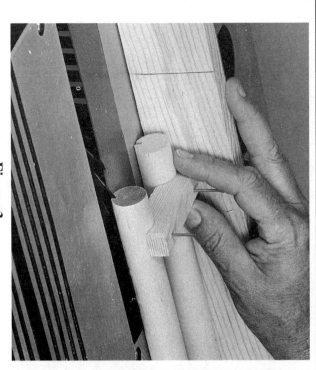

Figure 3.
Cut grooves into the supports (T) with the aid of the holding jig. Two are required to hold two dowels in place. Drive finishing nails partially into the dowel.

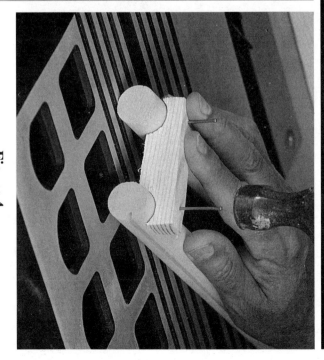

Figure 4.
After cutting one groove into each of the two dowels, remove the finishing nails and turn the dowels to their proper angles. Then cut the second groove where necessary.

properly. Glue all 1 in. dowels and the two 11½ in. by ½ in. dowel dash supports (W) into the base.

ASSEMBLY. For final assembly, glue all of the pieces into position in the following order: Glue the side covers (Q) to the steering support plate (B); interior front cover panels (R); under dash short panels (P); hood sides (N); hood side caps (BB) into holes in 1 in. dowels; hood front (O) and front cross support (W).

Install the hood hinge (AA) without glue. Then glue the hood top (M) to the hinge (AA); front panels under windshield (S) and their caps (X); windshield (W).

Figure 5.
Carefully lay out the base (A) and cut out the pattern with a saber saw equipped with a plywood cutting blade.

This project is courtesy of Georgia-Pacific Corporation, 133 Peachtree St. N.E., P.O. Box 105605, Atlanta, GA 30348. How-to photographs are courtesy of Skil Corporation.

School Bus

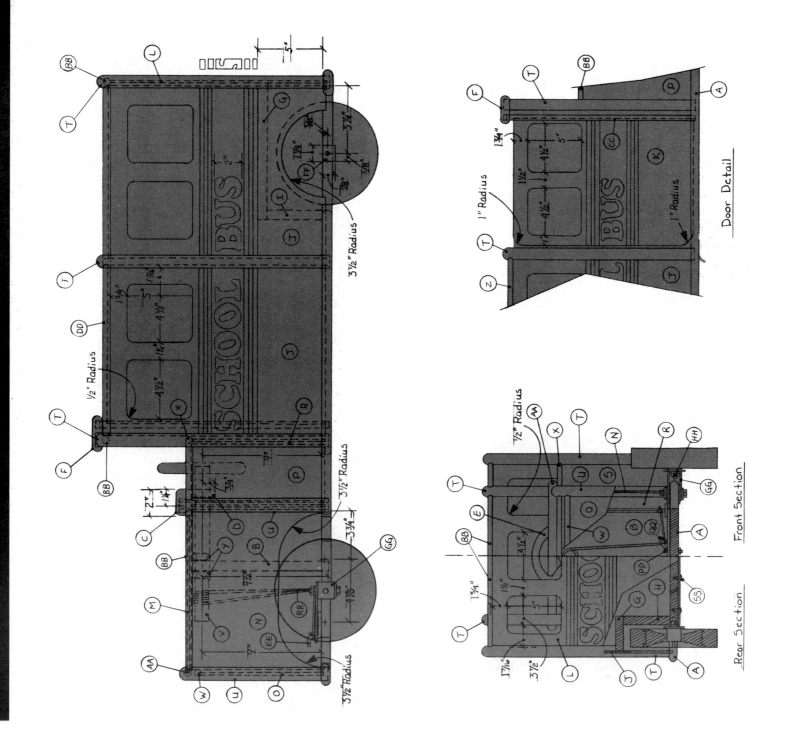

Door Detail

Front Section

Rear Section

98

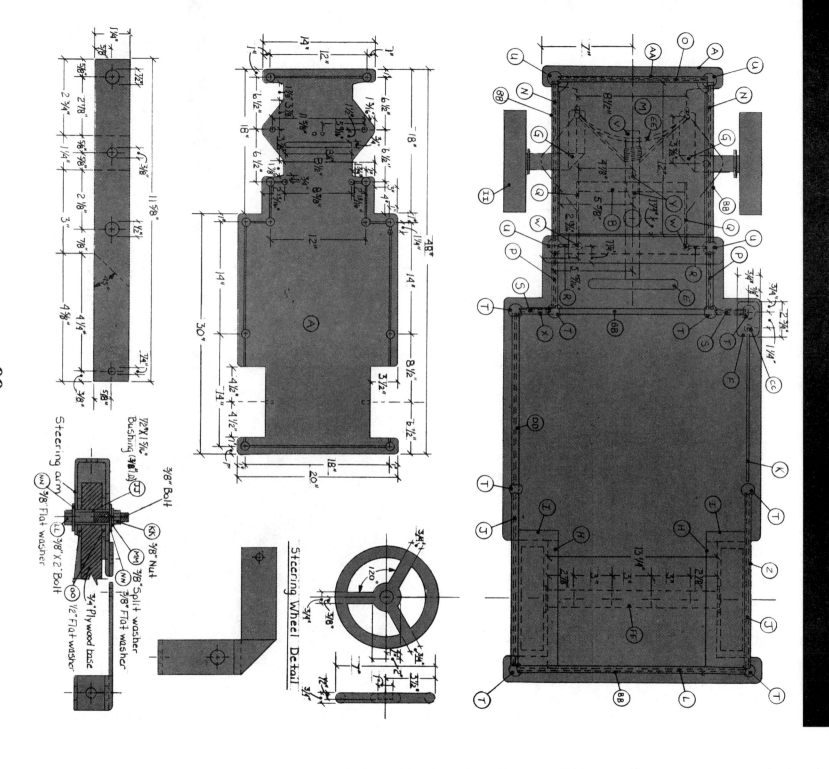

Steering Wheel Detail

Cutting List

3/4 in. AA Plywood

A	Base	48 x 20	1
B	Steering support plate	8¼ x 10¹¹⁄₁₆	1
C	Dash, top	14 x 2	1
D	Dash, front	11⅞ x 2¼	1
E	Steering wheel	7 dia.	1
F	Door hinge cap	2¾ x 1¾	1
G	Rear wheel cover, top	10¹¹⁄₁₆ x 3³⁄₁₆	2
H	Rear wheel cover, side	9¹⁵⁄₁₆ x 4¼	2
I	Rear wheel cover, front	4¼ x 3³⁄₁₆	2

1/8 in. Hardboard

J	Side panel	13⅜ x 16¾	3
K	Door panel	11¾ x 16¾	1
L	Rear panel	17⅜ x 16¾	1
M	Hood top	12 x 11¼	1
N	Hood side	12⅜ x 10⅜	2
O	Hood front	11⅜ x 9⅝	1
P	Short panel, under dash	4⅜ x 10⅜	2
Q	Side cover, steering support plate	4⅞ x 10³⁄₁₆	2

frame top (BB); left side panel (J) and its cap (DD); right side panel (J) and its cap (Z); rear panel (L) and its cap (BB); and dash assembly.

Place the door hinge (CC) in position in the base. Glue the door hinge cap (F) onto the 1 in. dowel only. Glue the door panel (K) to the hinge (CC).

Insert the steering wheel/column assembly through the hole in the dash front and the steering support plate. Glue the lock pins (Y) into the column on either side of the steering support plate (B). Wrap the ⅛ in. nylon cord around the steering column, directly over the small pulleys. Staple the center wrap of the cord into the column, pass the ends through the pulleys and tie the cord to the ends of the steering tie rod (EE) that protrudes through the steering arms.

Attach the front wheels to the steering arms (GG). Pass the shoulder bolts (HH) through each front wheel and through the ½ in. flat washer, steering arm and ⅜ in. split washer. Attach and tighten the ⅜ in. nut. Attach the rear wheels. Pass the shoulder bolt through

the wheel, the ½ in. flat washer, the rear axle strap and the ⅜ in. nut embedded in the base. Tighten them. Align the front wheel toe-in by bending the steering tie rod (EE).

FINISHING. What school bus would be complete without the traditional bright yellow paint and black lettering! Apply a latex paint sealer to the proj-

Figure 6.
Drill the 1 in. diameter holes for the supports (T) using a Forstner bit installed in a drill press.

R	Interior front cover, panel	1¼ x 10¾	2
S	Front panel under windshield	2⅜ x 10⅜	2
1 in. Dia. Dowels			
T	Support, tall	17⅞	8
U	Support, short	11½	4
V	Steering column	12	1
1/2 in. Dia. Dowels			
W	Dash support front cross support	11½	2
	front cross support	11½	1
X	Cap, front panel under windshield	2½	2
Y	Lock pin, steering column	1¼	2
Z	Cap, right side panel	13½	1
AA	Hood hinge	11⁷⁄16	1
BB	Hood side cap	17½	2
	rear panel cap	17½	1
	windshield frame top	17½	1
CC	Door hinge	17⁹⁄16	1
DD	Cap, left side panel	27½	1

Hardware			
EE	Steering tie rod	15 x ¼ metal rod	1
FF	Rear axle strap	14¾ x 1¼ x ⅛ steel bar	1
GG	Steering arm	11⅝ x 1¼ x ⅛ steel bar	2
HH	Shoulder bolt	⅜ x 2¼	4*
II	Wheel	8 x 1¾ (½ bore)	4
JJ	Bushing	1⁵⁄16 x ½ (⅜ I.D.) brass or steel	2
KK	Nut	⅜	6
LL	Bolt	⅜ x 2	2
MM	Split washer	⅜	4
NN	Flat washer	⅜	4
OO	Flat washer	½	8
PP	Eyebolt	¼ x 1	2
QQ	Pulley, small		2
RR	Nylon cord	36 x ⅛	1
SS	Screw, panhead	8 x ¾	4

Miscellaneous: wood glue; yellow paint (Krylon spray, color: school bus yellow); contact paper or vinyl self-stick shelf liner, Black (for stripes and letters: Cooper Black 2" height); finishing nails

Note: All dimensions are in inches.

*Shoulder: ½ x 1½

ect. When the sealer coat has dried, give the project a light sanding. Then apply one or two coats of a bright yellow gloss latex paint.

You can either paint on the letters and rules or purchase them from an art supply store.

SAFETY FIRST. Because this project is for little people, make sure all showing edges are rounded and sanded smooth. Any protruding part can, of course, cause injuries. If the bus will be transported down a hallway or out into the living room, you might want to consider putting rubber bumpers all around. These bumpers are similar to those found on your vacuum cleaner.

❖

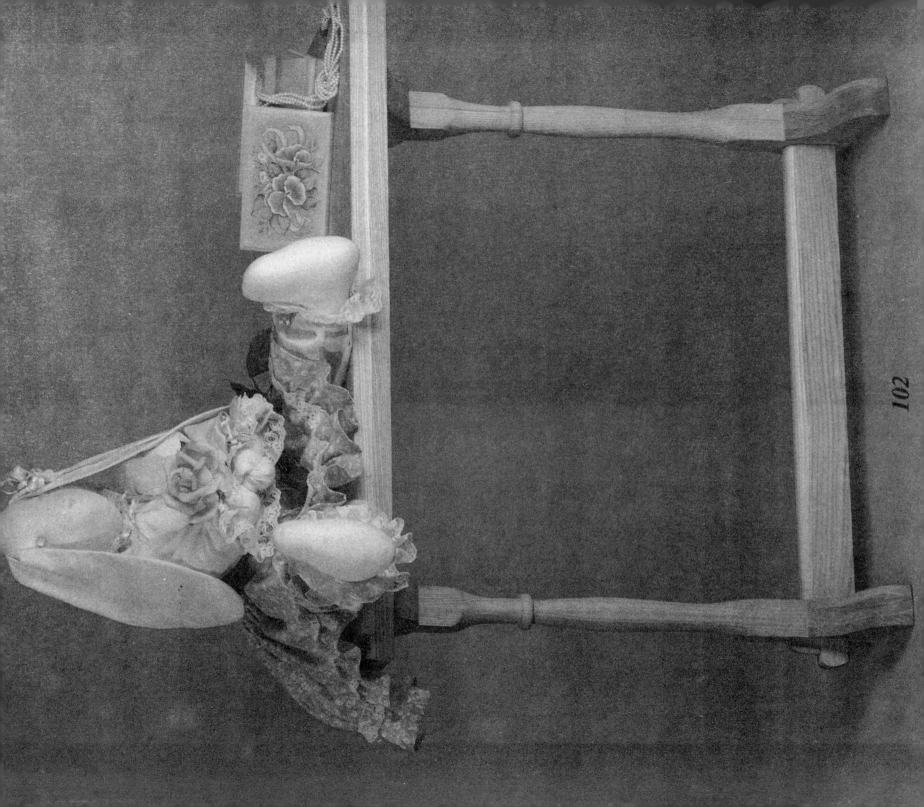

Hall Table

Built of solid ash, this classic hall table will last a lifetime. Mortise and tenon joints make this two-legged table sturdy, and the special foot design keeps the table from wobbling. This particular design is a replica of an existing table that was built approximately 60 years ago. Even after 60 years of wear and tear, the original hall table is still solid. A few nicks and scratches are the only visible signs of its many years of service.

SKILL LEVEL. This hall table is best suited to advanced woodworkers who have experience in making mortises and tenons. However, intermediate-level woodworkers should be able to tackle the project if they have access to a lathe and a table saw and are willing to learn how to cut mortises.

TIPS. A table of this style requires the use of select lumber. Walnut, mahogany and even oak are suitable construction materials.

CONSTRUCTION. Carefully cut out all of the project parts to their overall widths and lengths. You may have to edge-glue several narrower pieces of

The elegant, graceful lines of this hall table conceal its sturdiness. It will make a beautiful addition to your foyer, living room or dining room and will provide years of service.

wood stock in order to obtain the 12 in. width required for the top (A).

When edge-gluing the top, use a portable plane with a guide and cut the surface in one long, continuous stroke. Check the edges to make sure that there are no gaps and to guarantee that the workpieces to be glued will form a flat plane.

Edge-glue the workpieces that form the top with a good carpenter's glue (yellow glue). Use bar clamps to secure the workpieces, and allow the glue to dry for 24 hours.

Edge-glue the workpieces to form the legs (D). Use C-clamps to securely clamp the surfaces during the gluing process. After the glue has dried, cut the widths of the legs slightly oversize. Then use your portable plane to smooth the legs to their final dimension. Now, crosscut the legs to their proper lengths.

Cut the top (A) to its appropriate width and length on your table saw using a hollow-ground planer blade.

Miter the front and back rails (B) and the two side rails (C) on your power miter box. Secure these rails to the underside of the tabletop with glue and No. 8

Figure 1.

Lay out the foot pattern (G) on a wood blank, but do not cut out the pattern at this time. Instead, form the tenon that will fit into the mortise of the leg (D). Install a dado blade on your table saw and mill three edges to form the tenon. Then smooth the tenon cuts with a wide wood chisel.

Figure 2.

Form the stretcher (E) tenons on your table saw. Make repetitive cuts as shown and then smooth the tenon with a sharp, wide wood chisel.

Figure 3.

Locate the areas to be mortised on the stretcher (E), and then make repetitive holes with a Forstner bit installed in a drill press. Work carefully to avoid blemishing the stretcher (E) mortises.

by 1¼ in. flathead wood screws. Predrill all screw holes and countersink them so that the screw heads are flush with the surface of the wood.

Locate the areas to be mortised on each of the two legs (D). Then set up your table saw to the appropriate width and make stopped cuts into each of these mortise locations. Square the cuts with a sharp wood chisel. Make sure that the leg is securely clamped while finishing the mortise cut. Conclude the milling of the legs by turning them on your lathe, using the pattern shown in the illustration. Do your finish sanding on the lathe, too, using thin strips of sandpaper.

Glue material to make up the feet (G) and braces (F). Cut each workpiece to length and width. Lay out the designs for the foot (G) and the brace (F) workpieces, but do not cut them out at this time. Instead, form the tenons. Use a table saw equipped with a dado blade to form the main tenon. This requires cuts on the two wide edges and on one of the narrow edges.

104

Figure 4.
Joint the edges of the top (A) with a portable power plane.

Cutting List

A	Top	3/4 x 12 x 30	1
B	Front/back rail	3/4 x 3/4 x 30	2
C	Side rail	3/4 x 3/4 x 12	2
D	Leg	1 3/4 x 1 3/4 x 23	2
E	Stretcher	1 1/4 x 2 1/4 x 26 3/4	1
F	Brace	1 3/4 x 2 3/4 x 4 1/8	4
G	Foot	1 3/4 x 3 1/2 x 4 1/2	4
H	Key	1/2 x 3/4 x 3 1/8	2

Note: All material is ash unless otherwise indicated. All dimensions are in inches.

Practice making the cuts on scrap material first, test-fitting the tenon into the leg mortise. Once the saw is set properly, cut the tenons. Smooth the cut edge, if necessary, with a wood chisel so the mortise and tenon joint is snug. Keep in mind that there should be a gap of about 1/16 in. between the base of the mortise and the end of the tenon. This 1/16 in. gap allows for excess glue.

Test-fit all of the mortise and tenon joints, and then cut the foot and brace workpieces with a band saw. Finish sand the edges with a stationary belt sander.

Next, locate and cut the mortise that goes into the bottom of the leg assembly. This mortise will accommodate the stretcher (E). Drill a hole into the area to be mortised and then follow this up by cutting out the basic rectangle with a saber saw. Use a wide blade and make sure that the saw is cutting perpendicularly. Also, do not cut directly to the line; instead, stop short of the line. Now, use a wide, sharp wood chisel to square the cut.

Rout a design into the edge of the stretcher, as shown in the illustration, using a router bit installed in your router table. Next, form the tenons on your table saw. To do this, install a dado blade in your table saw and make repetitive cuts to the proper depths until you have milled out the tenons. Again, use a wide, sharp wood chisel to smooth out the cuts.

A key (H) will fit into a mortise cut into the stretcher (E). Locate the mortises for the two keys (H) into the tenons that you cut into the stretcher (E). Use a Forstner bit installed in a drill press, and make repetitive cuts in the area to be mortised. Work carefully, and square the cut with a wood chisel. Form the rounded end of the stretcher tenon by shaping it on a stationary disk sander.

Lay out the design of the keys and shape them on your stationary disk sander. Also, do the finish sanding at this time, making sure that the keys fit loosely into the stretcher's mortises.

ASSEMBLY. Finish sand all of the project parts until you achieve a smooth finish.

How-to photographs are courtesy of Skil Corporation.

Hall Table

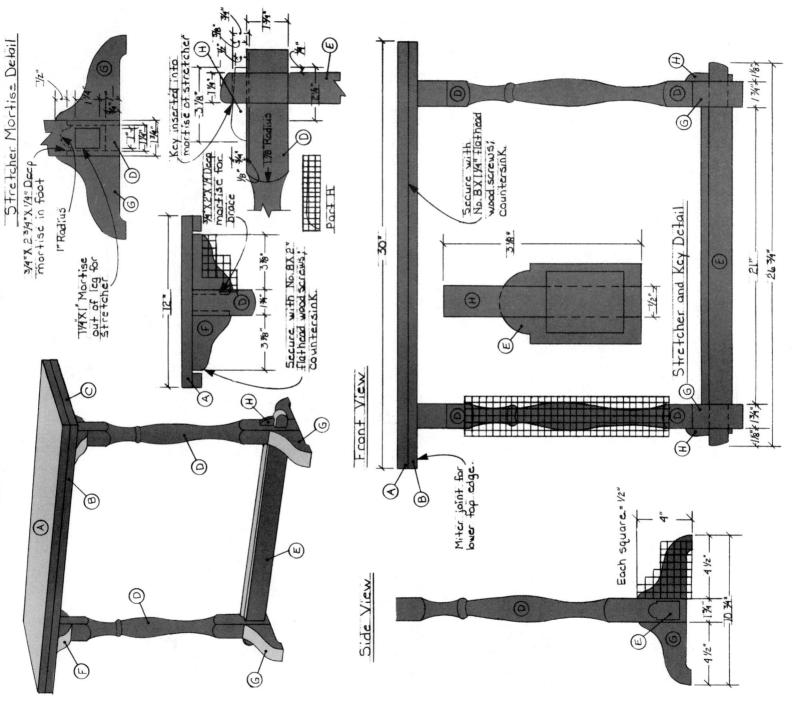

Stretcher Mortise Detail

3/4"X 2 3/4"X 1/4" Deep
mortise in foot

1" Radius

1/2"

1 1/4"

1/2"

3/4"

1/2"

1 3/4"

1 3/4" X 1" Mortise
out of leg for
stretcher.

1/2" X 2" X 1" Deep
mortise for
brace

Secure with No.8X 2"
Flathead wood screws;
Countersink.

12"

3 3/8"

1 3/4"

3 3/8"

Key inserted into
mortise of stretcher

3/8"

1 1/4"

1 1/4"

7 3/4"

3/4"

1/2"

5/8"

7/8" Radius

1/8"

3/4"

Part H

Front View

30"

Secure with
No. 8X 1 1/4" Flathead
wood screws;
Countersink.

3/8"

1/2"

1 1/8" 1 3/4"

1 3/4" 1 1/8"

1 3/4" 1 1/8"

21"

26 3/4"

Stretcher and Key Detail

Miter joint for
lower top edge.

Side View

Each square = 1/2"

4"

4 1/2"

4 1/2"

1 3/4"

10 3/4"

106

Figure 5.

Use a stationary disk sander to form the contours at the stretcher (E) ends. Take long, smooth strokes.

Glue each foot and brace to the legs with carpenter's glue. Make sure that the plane on which each foot and brace rests is absolutely flat. Allow the glue to dry.

Insert the stretcher into the leg mortises and lightly tap in the keys with a wood mallet.

Rest the tabletop upside down on a workbench and place the upper portion of the legs in place. The legs are attached to the tabletop with one No. 8 by 2 in. flathead wood screw driven into each of the four braces (F). Predrill these holes and countersink the screw heads. Then secure the assembly with glue and screws. Make sure that the unit remains absolutely square throughout this process.

FINISHING. After the glue has dried, finish sand the entire project. Then remove all fine dust particles with a damp, clean cloth.

Remove the two keys and apply a good coat of sealer to the entire project, including the underside of the tabletop. Allow the sealer coat to dry thoroughly before giving it a light sanding. Follow this with one or two applications of a satin varnish or polyurethane. Make sure that you sand between coats. When the project is dry, reinstall the keys.

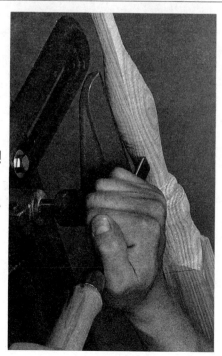

Figure 6.

Mark the contour points on the legs (D) after you have rounded the appropriate area. Then use a parting tool combined with calipers to set the turning diameters. Turn the areas with the aid of a sharp wood gouge.

Figure 7.

Use long strips of sandpaper to sand the legs on your lathe. Here we have used strips of sandpaper torn from a belt sander. As always, make sure that you wear adequate eye protection and a good dust mask.

Deluxe Headboard

Transform an ordinary bed into a streamlined unit with endless display and storage possibilities.

any people invest in a good-quality mattress and box spring but put off completing their bedroom set until the rest of the house is furnished. Well, wait no further. With this plan, you'll get a deluxe headboard, dresser and nightstand all rolled into one, with the added bonus of bookshelves, at a reasonable price.

SKILL LEVEL. This project is quite suitable for moderate-level woodworkers and ambitious beginners.

TIPS. Begin by measuring your bed. A regular full-size mattress measures about 54 in. by 75 in., a queen-size bed measures 60 in. by 80 in. and a king-size bed measures 76 in. by 80 inches. Be sure to allow extra space for sheets and other bedding and for clearance for your hands while making the bed. This unit was designed to accommodate a queen-size bed. You also will need to consider the height of your bed. Most bed frames rest on a steel frame with casters.

You may want to make the end units narrower or wider, depending on the wall space available in your bedroom.

CONSTRUCTION. This project is made up of three units: a central headboard and two vertical end units. You will need to construct the headboard and the units in your workshop and assemble them in your bedroom.

Central Headboard. Begin with the central headboard. After determining the width of the headboard, cut out all of the project parts to their overall widths and lengths. Use a power circular saw equipped with a plywood cutting blade, and cut with the good side down. Next, dado and rabbet the two side workpieces (A) with a router. Equip the router with a ¾ in. straight bit, and guide the tool along a straightedge to ensure a straight cut. Readjust the dado blade to make a ¼ in. wide by ⅜ in. deep cut. Then cut rabbets into both side workpieces as well as the top workpiece (F).

Secure the central headboard with carpenter's glue and 4d finishing nails. Sink all nailheads and fill in the blemishes with a good wood filler.

You will have to custom cut the back (D) from two sheets of ¾ in. plywood. The two sheets should form a seam at the lower shelf (P). After cutting the back workpieces, attach them to the central headboard with carpenter's glue and 4d finishing nails. Make sure that the assembly is square, and allow the glue to dry before you actually move the unit to your bedroom.

109

Figure 1.

Use a T-square to help you guide the router when dadoing the side workpieces (B) for the end units. Make progressively deeper passes until you achieve the final depth of cut.

Figure 2.

Cut a groove along the full length of the drawer fronts/backs (K) and sides (L) to accommodate the drawer bottoms (M). If you do not have a dado blade, readjust the fence position on progressive passes until you achieve the appropriate width.

End Units. Cut all of the end unit parts, with the exception of the drawers, to their overall widths and lengths.

Cut dadoes into the side workpieces (B), and then cut rabbets the full length of the sides (B) and the top workpieces (G).

Next, cut notches in the drawer unit top (H) so it will be flush with the outside of the sides (B).

Then assemble each of the side units with carpenter's glue and 4d finishing nails. Secure the top (G), side shelves (Q), drawer unit top (H), rails (I) and bottom workpieces (R) to the sides (B).

Now, cut and install the backs (E) to the unit with glue and finishing nails. Make sure that the unit is square and rests on a flat surface. Sink all nailheads

110

Locate the areas where the drawer pulls are to be installed and then slightly counterbore these areas, drilling from the inside of the drawer faces (J). Use a large diameter Forstner bit. This will prevent the fasteners from protruding beyond the surface of the drawer faces when secured to the drawer fronts (K).

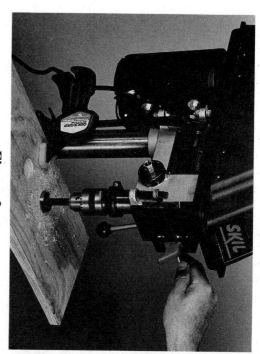

Figure 3.

and fill in any blemishes in the wood with an appropriate wood filler.

Drawers. Custom cut the drawers to suit the drawer openings. We designed the drawers to work in concert with 14 in. drawer glides. We suggest that you buy the drawer hardware before you actually cut out the drawer, because the side clearances for this type of specialty hardware will vary from manufacturer to manufacturer.

Rabbet the drawer fronts and backs (K) on your table saw. Then cut a groove the full length of each front and back as well as the drawer sides (L) to accommodate the drawer bottoms. Assemble the drawers with 4d finishing nails and carpenter's glue. Do not use glue to install the drawer bottoms. Square the assembly and allow the glue to dry. Finally, custom cut the drawer faces (J) and drill holes for the drawer pulls (N).

FINISHING. Finish sand the entire project, making sure to dull all edges and to fill in any gaps with a suitable wood filler.

Carefully remove all dust from the project. Take your time with this important step. Begin with a vacuum and then finish with a damp (but not wet), clean cloth.

This project is courtesy of Georgia-Pacific Corporation. 133 Peachtree St. N.E., P.O. Box 105605, Atlanta, GA 30348. How-to photographs are courtesy of Skil Corporation.

Cutting List

A	Side	3/4 x 11 x 72	2
B	Side	3/4 x 11 x 45	4
C	Side	3/4 x 18 x 26¼	4
D	Back	¼ x 63¼ x 71⅝	1
E	Back	¼ x 19¼ x 71⅝	2
F	Top	3/4 x 11 x 63¼	1
G	Top	3/4 x 11 x 19¼	2
H	Drawer unit top	3/4 x 19¼ x 20	2
I	Rail	3/4 x 3 x 18½	4
J	Drawer face	3/4 x 7¾ x 18¼	6
K	Drawer front/back	3/4 x 7¾ x 17½	12
L	Drawer side	3/4 x 7¾ x 15¾	12
M	Drawer bottom	¼ x 15¾ x 16½	6
N	Pull	½ x 1¼ x 1	6
O	Drawer glide	½ x 3/4 x 16	12
P	Long shelf	3/4 x 10¾ x 63¼	2
Q	Side shelf	3/4 x 10¾ x 19¼	4
R	Bottom	3/4 x 3 x 19¼	2

Note: All material is plywood unless otherwise indicated. All dimensions are in inches.

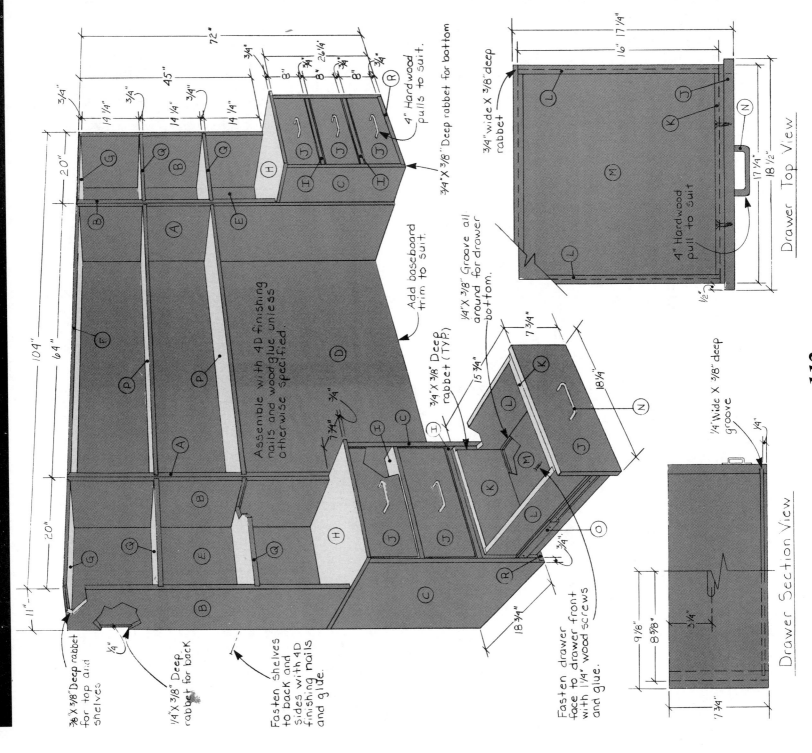

Deluxe Headboard

72"

45"

3/4"

8" 26 1/4" 8"

3/4" 3/4" 3/4" 3/4"

R

4" Hardwood pulls to suit.

3/4" X 3/8" Deep rabbet for bottom

14 1/4" 14 1/4" 14 1/4"

3/4" 3/4" 3/4"

20"

G Q B Q H

J J J

H C H

3/4" X 3/8" Deep rabbet

16" 17 1/4"

L

K J

N

4" Hardwood pull to suit

3/4" wide X 3/8" deep rabbet

18 1/4"

17 1/4"

Drawer Top View

1/2"

B A E

104"

64"

Add baseboard trim to suit.

Assemble with 4D finishing nails and woodglue unless otherwise specified.

F P A

1/4" X 3/8" Groove all around for drawer bottom.

7 3/4"

K

L

N

3/4" X 3/8" Deep rabbet (TYP.)

15 3/4"

18 1/4"

1/4" wide X 3/8" deep groove

1/4"

D

7 3/4" 3/4"

H C H

M

K

L

J

G Q E Q

20"

H

J J

B

11"

1/4"

3/8" X 3/8" Deep rabbet for top and shelves

1/4" X 3/8" Deep rabbet for back

Fasten shelves to back and sides with 4D finishing nails and glue.

C

R

O

3/4"

Fasten drawer face to drawer front with 1 1/4" wood screws and glue.

18 3/4"

9/8"

8 5/8"

3/4"

1 3/4"

Drawer Section View

112

It is imperative that you apply a good paint sealer before you paint the unit; otherwise the wood grain will absorb your final paint unevenly. Depending on the type of paint you apply, the wood grain also may rise, resulting in a rough surface.

After the sealer coat has dried, sand the entire project. Again, take your time in removing any sanding residue. Apply a coat of your favorite color or colors, and follow this up with at least one more coat. Make sure that you sand in between coats.

INSTALLATION. Remove the base trim from the area where the central headboard is to be installed. Attach the central unit to the bedroom wall with 1½ in. drywall screws, countersinking the screw heads. Make sure that you drive the screws into wall studs.

Secure the end units to the wall in a similar fashion, and then attach them to the central unit with 1¼ in. drywall screws. Make sure that you clamp the surfaces to be joined before driving in the drywall screws.

Cut the base trim you removed earlier so it will fit between the wall and the end units and also within the base of the central headboard.

Install the drawers and the drawer glides, and then attach the drawer faces with 1¼ in. drywall screws driven from inside the drawer fronts.

Next, attach the front of the metal bed frame to the wall with an appropriate fastener. You probably will have to predrill holes to accept wall anchors before securing the bed frame.

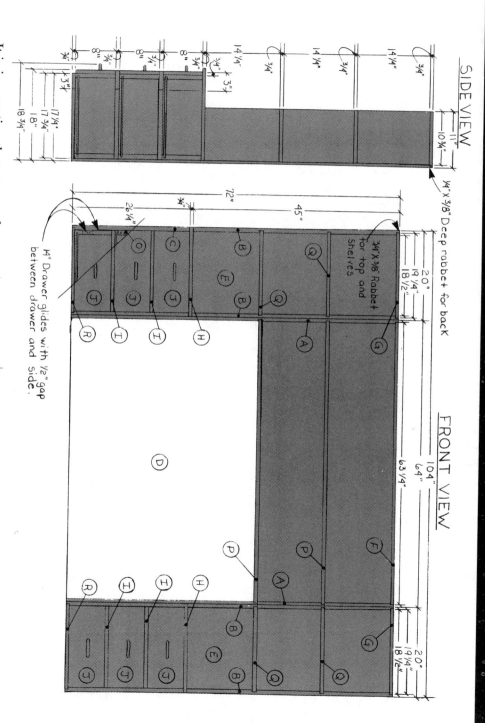

113

❖

Pine Desk

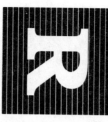

Roomy drawers and a covered desk provide the perfect ingredients for a tidy but functional piece of furniture. Our pine desk will look great in your dining room, living room or even master bedroom. Its greatest asset is that it hides the clutter!

SKILL LEVEL. This is a great project for intermediate-level woodworkers. However, beginners may want to tackle this project if they are confident in making dadoes and have access to either a table saw or a router. If not, butt joints can be substituted for the dadoes, but the dimensions will have to be adjusted.

TIPS. Just about any kind of wood can be used to build the desk. We used No. 2 pine, but grainy woods such as oak and ash are other outstanding choices.

CONSTRUCTION. Cut out all of the project parts, with the exception of the drawer workpieces, to their overall widths and lengths. Use a hollow-ground planer blade on your table saw to obtain an ultrasmooth finish cut.

Lay out the top angle in the side workpieces (A), and cut it out with a power circular saw guided by a straightedge.

Reminiscent of an antique secretary, this little pine desk takes up little space yet offers lots of room to work.

Using your table saw, cut the 20 degree bevel at the back of the top workpiece (B), both rails (I, J), the door (H) and the front edge of the desk top (G). Make sure that you use guides to cut the narrower rail (J). If you do not have the proper guides, cut a bevel into the edge of a wider piece of material and then rip the material to the appropriate width.

Now, install a dado blade and cut rabbets into the back inside edge of the two side workpieces (A).

With the table saw blade still tilted at 20 degrees, make a stopped rabbet at the back of the top workpiece (B). Make repetitive cuts in order to achieve the ¼ in. depth of cut. When finished, square the cut with a wood chisel.

Readjust the dado blade to cut a ¾ in. wide by ¾ in. deep rabbet into each of the side workpieces. Make your cuts using a miter gauge to ensure that the dado is precisely at a right angle.

Assemble the desk using carpenter's glue and 4d finishing nails. Attach the three shelves (E), the desk top support (F), the desk top (G) and the top (B) to one another. Square the assembly, and allow the glue to dry for 24 hours before proceeding with the next step.

115

Figure 1.

If you do not have a table saw, you can cut the dadoes into the side workpieces (A) using a router equipped with a ³/₄ in. rabbeting bit. Guide the router along a straightedge and hold the tool firmly.

Once the glue has dried, attach the two rails (I, J) underneath the top workpiece (B).

Insert the door (H) and check for clearance. You probably will have to trim the sides of the door and perhaps the top edge. Ideally, you should have a ⅛ in. clearance at the top and at both sides. When everything is perfect, install the door with a continuous hinge and two 7 in. combination hinges or drop-leaf hinges. If you use a combination hinge, you will have to mortise an area out so that the mounting hardware is flush with the work surfaces.

Rout a ³/₈ in. cove into the edge of the top rail (C), using a router table. Install the rail to the top workpiece (B) with glue and finishing nails. Predrill the nail holes to prevent wood splitting.

Attach the back (D) to the back of the assembly with carpenter's glue and small brads. Remember to drive the brads into the top workpiece (B) at an angle.

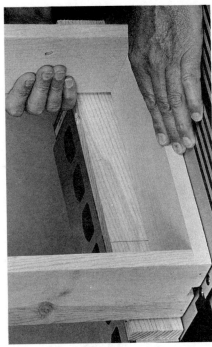

Figure 2.

Again, if you do not have a table saw to cut the grooves into the drawer workpieces (K, L), install a ¹/₄ in. straight bit in your router and use your router's edge guide as shown to mill the grooves.

Figure 3.

Here we are using a table saw to cut grooves into the assembled drawer. The table saw is set to cut a ³/₄ in. wide groove. If you use a router, the drawer and the straight-edge must be securely attached to the workbench. During the drawer assembly, note that any nails must be driven in areas other than those to be mortised.

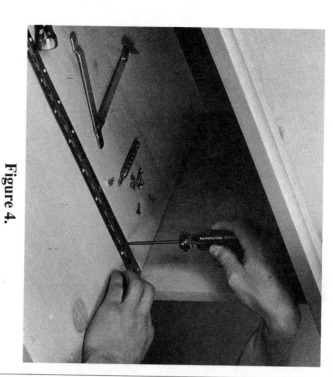

Figure 4.

Attach the door (H) to the desk top (G) with a continuous hinge.

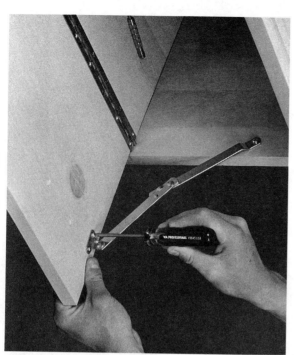

Figure 5.

The type of drop leaf you use is optional. You can use a 7 in. combination hinge, or the drop-leaf hardware that we used. Various types are available at your local hardware store or lumberyard.

Cutting List

A	Side	3/4 x 14 x 43	2
B	Top	3/4 x 16 x 30	1
C	Top rail	3/4 x 1 1/2 x 30	1
D	Back	1/4 x 27 1/4 x 43 3/8	1
		plywood	
E	Shelf	3/4 x 13 3/4 x 27 1/4	3
F	Desk top		
	support	3/4 x 3 x 27 1/4	1
G	Desk top	3/4 x 12 7/8 x 27 1/4	1
H	Door	3/4 x 11 1/4 x 26 1/4	1
I	Rail	3/4 x 1 1/2 x 26 1/2	1
J	Rail	3/4 x 3/4 x 26 1/2	1
K	Drawer front/		
	face/back	3/4 x 47/8 x 26 1/8	9
L	Drawer side	3/4 x 47/8 x 12 1/4	6
M	Drawer bottom	1/4 x 12 1/4 x 25 3/8	3
		plywood	
N	Drawer runner	3/4 x 1/2 x 13 maple	6

Note: All material is pine unless otherwise indicated. All dimensions are in inches.

Measure the inside drawer cavities and custom cut these if necessary. Variances in the depth of the dado cuts that you made and in wood thickness may result in dimensions that are different from ours. Now, rip the main drawer workpieces (K, L) to their proper widths, and then crosscut them to their correct lengths.

Dado the drawer backs and the drawer fronts to accommodate the drawer sides. Follow this up by grooving the inside bottom of all of the drawer work-

117

Pine Desk

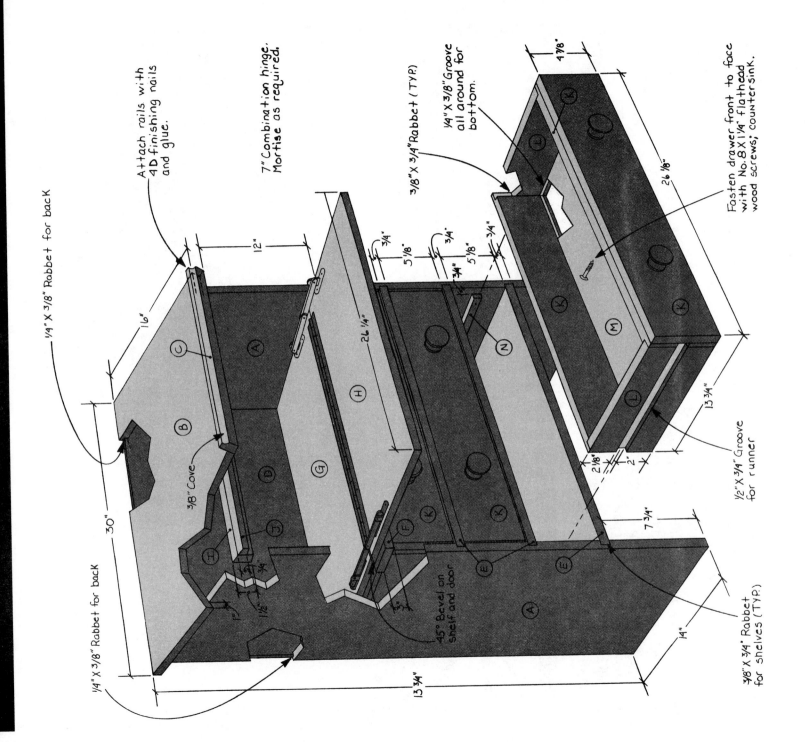

Attach rails with 4D finishing nails and glue.

7" Combination hinge. Mortise as required.

3/8" X 3/4" Rabbet (TYP)

1/4" X 3/8" Groove all around for bottom.

Fasten drawer front to face with No.8 X 1 1/4" flathead wood screws; countersink.

1/4" X 3/8" Rabbet for back

1/4" X 3/8" Rabbet for back

3/8" Cove

45° Bevel on shelf and door

1/2" X 3/4" Groove for runner

3/8" X 3/4" Rabbet for shelves (TYP)

12"

16"

30"

1"

1 1/2"

3/4"

5/8"

3/4"

3/4"

5/8"

26 1/4"

4 7/8"

26 1/8"

13 3/4"

2 1/8"

2"

7 3/4"

14"

13 3/4"

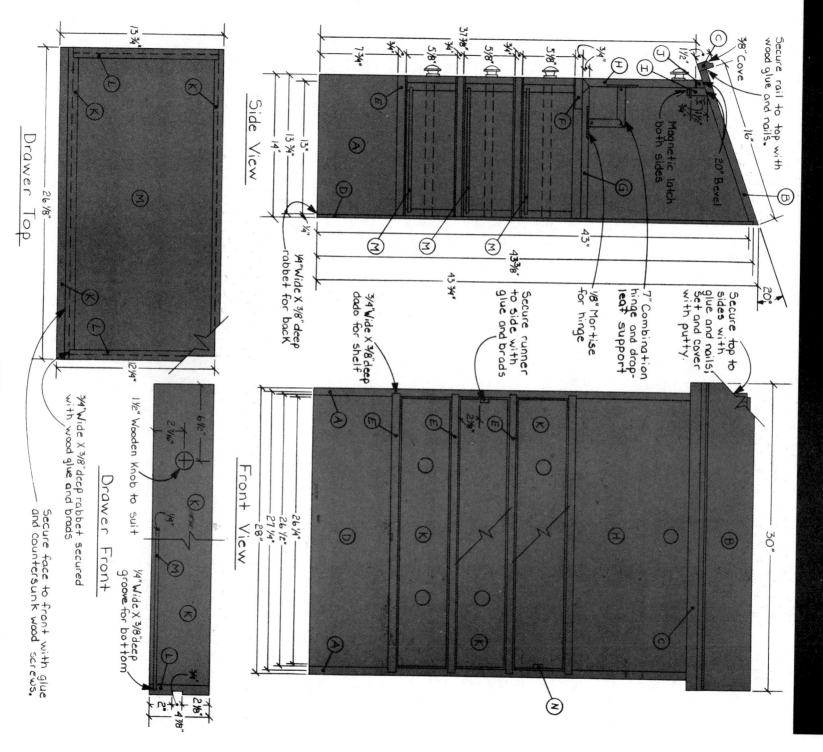

Side View

Secure rail to top with
wood glue and nails.

⅜" Cove

20° Bevel

Secure top to
sides with
glue and nails,
Set and cover
with putty.

Magnetic latch
both sides

⅛" Mortise
for hinge

7" Combination
hinge and drop-
leaf support

Secure runner
to side with
glue and brads

¾" Wide X ⅜" deep
dado for shelf

¼" Wide X ⅜" deep
rabbet for back

Front View

Drawer Top

Drawer Front

1½" Wooden Knob to suit

¼" Wide X ⅜" deep
groove for bottom

¾" Wide X ⅜" deep rabbet secured
with wood glue and brads

Secure face to front with glue
and countersunk wood screws.

119

pieces to accept the drawer bottoms (M). Now, custom cut the drawer bottoms to suit.

Glue up the drawer workpieces, with the exception of the drawer faces, using carpenter's glue and finishing nails. Do not glue the drawer bottoms (M), as this allows for expansion and contraction with temperature and humidity changes. Also, be careful not to drive nails into the areas that will be milled for the drawer runners (N). Square the assembly and let the glue cure for 24 hours.

Set your table saw's dado blade to cut a ¾ in. wide by ½ in. deep dado into the assembled drawer. Now, install the drawer runners (N) to the sides (A) with carpenter's glue and finishing nails. Double-check to make sure that the drawers fit inside the drawer cavities without binding.

Drill holes into the drawer faces and counterbore an area on the inside of each drawer face so that the knob's screw will be recessed. If you do not do this, the head of the screw will come in contact with the drawer front, resulting in a conspicuous gap. Fasten the drawer front to the drawer face with No. 8 by 1¼ in. flathead wood screws. Countersink the screw heads.

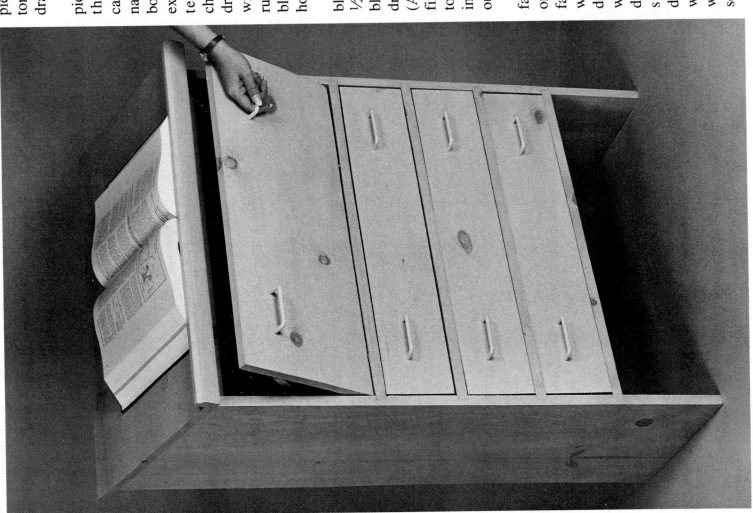

Figure 6.

Install magnetic door hinges at both ends of the unit. This keeps the door upright when it is in the closed position.

Drill a hole into the door (H) to install the remaining knob.

Install magnetic door hinges at both ends of the inside desk cavity so that the door will stay upright when closed.

FINISHING. Remove the knobs, the two 7 in. combination hinges and the continuous hinge. Then sink all nailheads and fill in with a nontoxic wood filler. Follow this up by finish sanding the entire project.

If you prefer, stain the project following the manufacturer's instructions for application. Follow this up by applying a satin finish polyurethane. Finish sand the dried coat before applying a final coat of polyurethane.

Reinstall the hardware and the knobs to complete your desk.

——— ❖ ———

Figure 7.

After predrilling the holes for the knobs, make sure that you counterbore an area for the knob screws so they do not interfere when the drawer faces are attached to the drawer fronts.

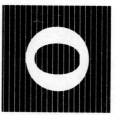

rganization is the key ingredient in any workshop. This handy saw blade holder is just the ticket for storing saw blades. There is nothing worse than a dull saw blade or not being able to find the right size blade when you need it. This saw blade holder will protect your blades and keep them organized, plus it will add a polished look to your workshop.

SKILL LEVEL. This is an ideal project for intermediate-level woodworkers, and it provides a nice, new challenge for beginning woodworkers.

TIPS. You will be using wood chisels to form a square mortise into each of the two side workpieces (B). It is a good idea to have a 1/4 in. wide wood chisel. These can be purchased at almost any home center or lumberyard. Make sure that the chisels are very sharp.

CONSTRUCTION. We used cherry and cherry plywood to construct the saw blade holder.

Note that the sides (B) and bottom (C) are milled with multiple grooves. Also, note that the sides have stopped grooves where the small dividers (E) are to be installed. Therefore, it is not a good idea to cut the workpieces to their overall length. Instead, rip a longer piece of cherry to the proper width and then lay out each of the workpieces on it. You will find that this is much easier than trying to mill a stopped groove into a smaller length of material on a table saw.

Set up your table saw to cut the proper width and depth when dadoing. Then determine the starting and stopping points for cutting a stopped groove. Do this using a scrap piece of material. Carefully lower the scrap material onto the rotating blade as the other end is held firmly to the tool's table. From this, put marks onto the fence guide to indicate where you should start and end your cuts.

Mill all of the grooves on the longer length of cherry material. When you are finished, crosscut the sides and the bottom to their respective lengths. Now, rabbet each of the side workpieces to accommodate the bottom workpiece.

Lay out the design in each of the large and small dividers (D, E), and then cut out the pattern on a scroll saw. Sand each of the contours with a drum sander installed in your drill press.

Lay out the handle contour in the handle workpiece (A). Bore two 3/4 in. diameter holes in the handhold area and then cut out the section in between with your scroll saw. Follow this up by cutting the contour on your scroll saw. Then sand the design with a drum sander.

Square the stopped grooves into each of the side workpieces with a 1/4 in. wide wood chisel. Then cut out the design and sand the edges.

Every woodworker will appreciate this handy blade caddy.

Saw Blade Holder

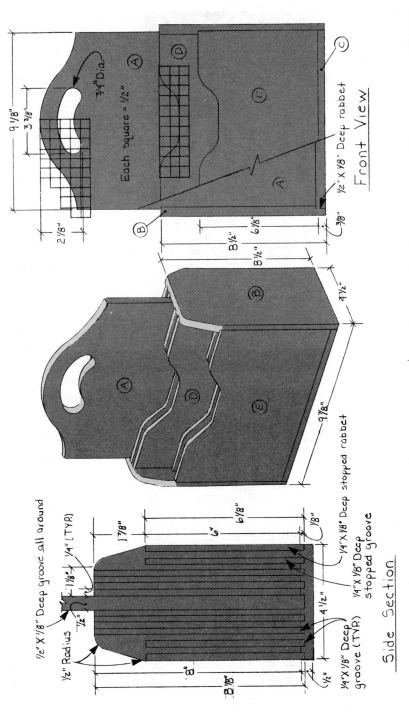

Front View

¾" Dia.
9⅛"
3⅜"
2⅛"
Each square = ½"
A
D
C
B
½" x ⅛" Deep rabbet
⅜"
6⅛"
8½"

A
B
D
E
8½"
4½"
9⅞"
½" x ⅛" Deep stopped rabbet

Side Section

½" x ⅛" Deep groove all around
1⅛"
¼" (TYP.)
1⅞"
6"
6⅛"
⅛"
½" Radius
½"
¼" x ⅛" Deep stopped groove
¼" x ⅛" Deep groove (TYP.)
4½"
8"
8⅛"
½"

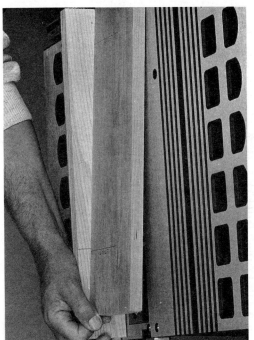

Figure 2.

Mark the stopping and cutting points on your longer piece of material for cutting the grooves in the sides (B) and the bottom (C). Slightly overshoot your beginning mark and lower the workpiece.

Figure 1.

The point at which the cutting tip of the saw blade begins to touch this scrap wood is where the cut needs to begin. Project this point onto the fence. In a similar manner, determine the tangent point where cuts should end.

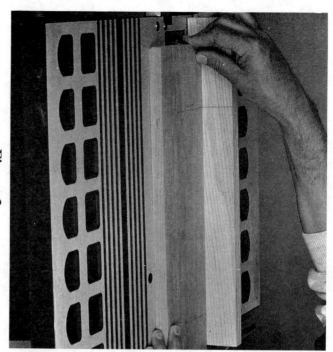

Figure 3.

Firmly hold your workpiece and back up the workpiece so that the beginning mark on your board coincides with the beginning mark on your fence. Do this slowly. Then finish the cut by moving the workpiece forward.

ASSEMBLY. The saw blade holder is assembled with glue. Before applying the glue, dry-assemble the unit, using clamps to hold everything together. You may need to sand or trim the pieces so that everything fits properly.

Once you are satisfied with the assembly, apply carpenter's glue to all of the grooves in the side workpieces as well as to the bottom workpiece. Secure the workpieces and install all of the dividers. Make sure that the assembly is square and that the joints are fairly tight. Allow the glue to cure for 24 hours.

FINISHING. You can either leave the project as is or apply a spray-on varnish. If you opt for one of the aerosol-type spray applications, give it at least two light coats of a satin finish polyurethane.

❖

Cutting List

A	Handle	½ x 9⅛ x 14¼		1
B	Side	½ x 4½ x 8½		2
C	Bottom	½ x 4½ x 9⅛		1
D	Large divider	¼ x 8⅛ x 9⅛	plywood	4
E	Small divider	¼ x 6⅛ x 9⅛	plywood	4

Note: All material is cherry unless otherwise indicated. All dimensions are in inches.

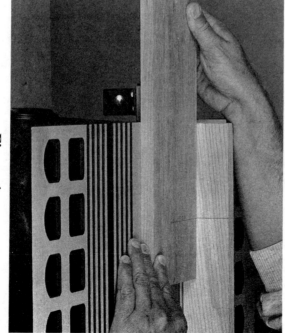

Figure 4.

Move the workpiece forward until the stopping mark coincides with the stopping mark on the fence. At this point, carefully turn off your machine. Remove the workpiece once the blade has stopped.

How-to photographs are courtesy of Skil Corporation and Vermont American Tool Company.

OUTDOOR PROJECTS

Trellis Gazebo

Enhance your outdoor entertaining with this beautiful redwood gazebo.

hether you are formally entertaining or just gathering together casually with family and friends, this gazebo creates a light and airy mood and an elegant, intimate atmosphere. The trellis-style roof lets sunlight filter into the covered area, while the open sides allow cool breezes to flow through.

For a firm base, we recommend building the gazebo on either a concrete slab or a wood deck.

SKILL LEVEL. Intermediate-level to advanced woodworkers should tackle this project. Experience with pouring concrete, leveling posts and cutting compound angles is necessary.

TIPS. Even the best of plans may call for on-site changes, particularly when larger structures such as this one are involved. Cut the workpieces as you go, because it is likely the structure will not be absolutely square. Therefore, compound angles may have to be reconfigured.

BUILDING PERMITS. Local and state codes probably will require a building permit, based upon this general plan and any other enhancements you may wish to make to your project — adding lighting, a patio or a deck, for example. Building permit officials will need to know where the gazebo and any enhancements are to be located on your property, how much the total

project will cost and when the project will be completed. Some municipalities may require that licensed professionals do part of the work.

LAYOUT. To make a concrete slab, level an area about 12 ft. square. Build a 10½ ft. square form of all-heart redwood 2x6 lumber. Nail the joints with 16d galvanized nails for weather resistance. Position the form on the site, digging shallow trenches to locate the top of the form 3½ in. above the grade. The form will remain in place, making an attractive border for the slab.

Check the squareness of the form before proceeding. Measure the diagonals in both directions. When they are equal, the form is square.

Level the form carefully using a long, straight 2x4 and a carpenter's level. For drainage, you may want to slope the slab slightly. If you do, make certain that the slope is even by checking the bubble on your level. Checked in the other direction, however, the forms should be level.

Cut points into the ends of the 2x2 stakes. You will need 24 stakes, 18 in. long. Drive the stakes spaced 2 ft. apart on the outside of the form. The tops of the stakes should be just below the top of the form to allow for easy finishing of the concrete. Avoid forcing the form inward, and do not nail the stakes to the form. This makes the stakes easy to remove later.

129

Trellis Gazebo

Locate the positions of the four corner posts on the inside of the form. Measure from the corners of the form, using nails to stretch string from corner to corner. The points at which the strings cross mark the center of each post. As you did with the form, measure the diagonals to make sure that your post positions are at the corners of a perfect square.

At each post position, dig a hole large enough to accommodate the post and its concrete footing. Then insert the four corner posts into the holes. Carefully position each of the posts and use supports to hold them upright. Drive double-headed nails through the supports and into the posts. This process makes removing the supports easier. Use a level to ensure that the posts are perfectly vertical.

Now, mix and pour concrete from premixed bags of cement that include aggregate. Pour the concrete so it is flush with the ground.

To reinforce the concrete slab (not the postholes) and to help prevent cracking, lay in 6-6-10-10 concrete reinforcing steel mesh. Position the steel mesh so it lies in the middle of the slab and is level, propping it up where necessary with small stones.

Add 1x3 dividers according to the pattern shown in the diagram, or create your own pattern. Toenail the dividers to the form, and prop them up with small stones to match the height of the perimeter form. Use all-heart redwood for these dividers to prevent water damage.

You will need approximately 1¾ cubic yards of concrete for a 12 ft. by 12 ft. slab. The job will be easier if you have a home center nearby that offers premixed concrete in trailers. Otherwise, you can mix the concrete yourself, or order it from a ready-mix concrete firm.

Pour the concrete into your prepared form, spreading it evenly. If necessary, press the steel mesh down into the wet concrete. Use a 14 ft. long 2x4 as a screed to level the surface. You will need another person to help you with this job. Work the 2x4 back and forth

across the form, moving slowly from one end of the slab to the other. Add concrete to any low spots you see. It will take two or three passes of the screed to level the concrete and make it even with the top of the form.

Allow the concrete to set slightly, then finish the surface with a wooden float. You can simplify this job by building a "bridge." Place a 2x12 on concrete blocks positioned outside the form. If you place this bridge across the center of the slab, you will be able to reach every part of the concrete.

The finish left by the float provides a nonskid surface, ideal for this type of structure. If you wish, however, you can smooth the surface even more by using a steel trowel after the concrete sets semihard. Another finishing option is to sweep the partially set concrete with a broom, which makes an attractive pattern.

Keep the new concrete damp for several days so that it will cure without cracking. Spray the new slab lightly with a garden hose or, even better, cover the new concrete with a sheet of plastic.

Once the concrete has cured, remove the outer stakes and begin building the gazebo. The posts, now in concrete footings, most likely are at different heights and must be trimmed so they are all topped at the same plane. To accomplish this, use a long, straight 2x4 with a level placed on top. Then mark one set of corner posts to the appropriate height. Move along the perimeter of the four posts, using the leveled 2x4 to locate the level plane and mark each post.

Lay out the 20 degree bevels required for the tops of the posts. Use a protractor, making sure the bevels are facing the correct way. Trim the tops of the four corner posts with a sharp handsaw.

Design and finish photo are courtesy of the California Redwood Association, 405 Enfrente Dr., Suite 200, Novato, CA 94949. How-to photographs are courtesy of Skil Corporation.

Next, cut four redwood 2x4s for the cross braces. Lay out the 1½ in. by 1¾ in. intersecting notches in the brace components, as shown in the diagram. Cut the notches with a saber saw. The notches should be exactly half the width of the lumber. Use a sharp chisel to remove the waste from the notches.

Assemble the brace structure by interlocking the notches. Add corner brackets to strengthen the assembly, attaching them with 6d galvanized nails.

Tack stop blocks of scrap lumber to the posts, lightly nailing the blocks 2 in. from the top of each post. These will hold the braces in place temporarily while you fasten them. With help, raise the braces into position. Adjust them to center the brace structure between the posts.

Bore pilot holes and fasten the braces to the corner posts with ¼ in. by 2½ in. lag screws. Use flat washers under the screw heads.

Now, cut the 2x6 rafters. Start by ripping two 19 degree bevels along the entire length of the upper surface of each rafter. Set your saw's depth of cut so that the bevels will intersect at the center of the rafter.

Cut the profiles of the rafter ends to the angles shown in the diagram. Cut the 70 degree angle on both ends first, then set the blade's bevel angle to 47 degrees to form the outer double bevel shown in the diagram. To save setup time, make each cut on all four rafters.

Assemble one pair of rafters with ⅜ in. by 4 in. lag screws. Counterbore the fastener holes to keep the screw heads below the surface. Lightly nail a length of 1x4 lumber to reinforce the rafter assembly temporarily. With help, position the rafter assembly on the posts, with the peak in the center. Use lag screws to attach the assembly to the braces. Add the remaining rafters, again fastening them with countersunk lag screws at the top joint. Nail the top joint where the four rafters meet with 16d nails.

Lay out and cut the angled braces to the dimensions provided in Detail 4. Once again, make match-ing cuts on each brace before changing your setup. Fasten these braces to the posts and rafters with ¼ in. by 3 in. lag screws. Again, counterbore for the screw heads.

Rip a 60 degree bevel on the top edge of the 2x6 stock to be used for the fascia boards. Measure each side of the structure carefully to allow for slight variations. Cut the trim to length, mitering the ends of each board at a 32½ degree bevel and 57¼ degree angle. Attach the trim to the rafters with 16d galvanized nails.

Now, add the drip rail trim to the structure. Cut the 2x4 stock to length, once again compound mitering the corners.

Complete the shelter by adding the 2x4 trellis boards to the roof. Start by tacking one board in

Shopping List

4x6 redwood	32 ft.
4x4 redwood	60 ft.
2x6 redwood	84 ft.
2x4 redwood	200 ft.
1x3 redwood	36 ft.
6 galvanized corner brackets	4
6-6-10-10 concrete reinforcing mesh	144 sq. ft.
¼ x 2½ carriage bolts	8
¼ x 2½ lag screws	36
¼ x 3 lag screws	8
6d, 16d galvanized siding nails	as needed
Wood sealer and preservative	as needed

Note: All material is redwood unless otherwise indicated. All dimensions are in inches.

Trellis Gazebo

See Detail 1 to determine compound miter.

2×4 (TYP.)

4×6 Beam (TYP.)

Fasten first trellis to border 2×6 with 16D galvanized nails.

Concrete foundation to suit building site

12" Dia. ×36" concrete pier. Follow local building codes.

Fasten trellis members with 16D galvanized siding nails.

4×4 See Detail 4 (TYP.)

Fasten trellis brace with ¼"×3" lag screws. 1" dia. ×1" deep recess.

4×4 × 8' Post

Galvanized corner brackets (TYP.). Fasten with 6D galvanized nails.

3½"

1½" (TYP.)

2×4 (TYP.)

Lap joints (TYP.)

Detail 2

4×6 Trellis beam

47°

72°

Detail 1

47°

70°

4×6 Trellis beam

Detail 3

132

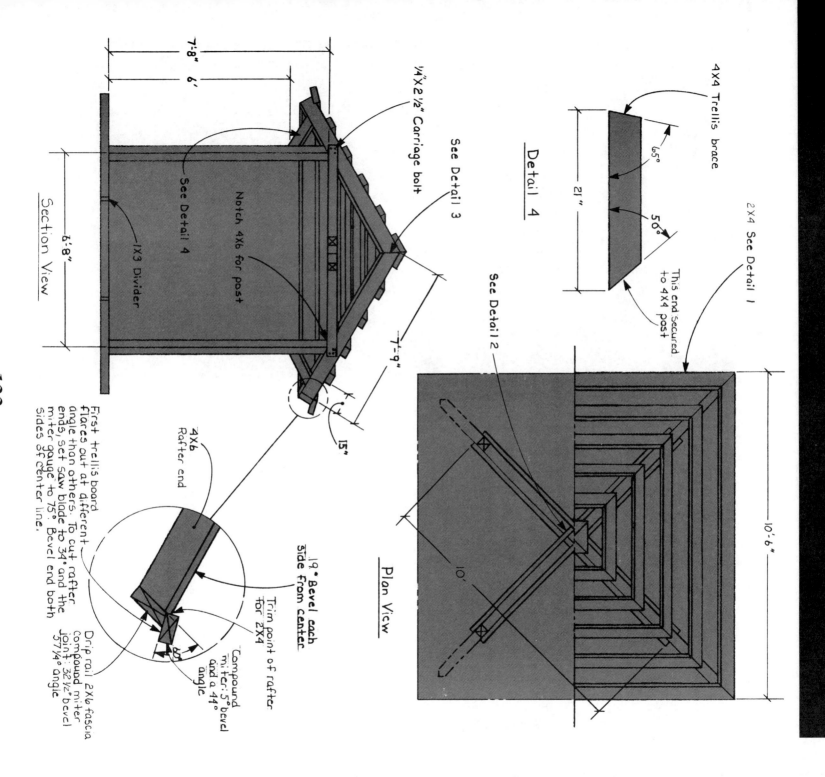

133

7'-8"

6'

1/4"X 2½" Carriage bolt

See Detail 3

See Detail 4

Notch 4X6 for post

1X3 Divider

Section View

6'-8"

15°

7'-9"

4X4 Trellis brace

Detail 4

65°

50°

21"

2X4 See Detail 1

This end secured to 4X4 post

See Detail 2

Plan View

10'-6"

10'

4X6 Rafter end

.19° Bevel each side from center

Trim point of rafter for 2X4

Compound miter: 5° bevel and a 44° angle

Drip rail 2X6 fascia compound miter joint: 32½° bevel 57¼° angle

First trellis board flares out at different angle than others. To cut rafter ends, set saw blade to 34° and the miter gauge to 75°. Bevel end both sides of center line.

DETERMINING AND CUTTING COMPOUND ANGLES

Figure 2.

Now mark the inside of the fascia board.

Figure 1.

To determine the compound cuts for the fascia boards, place a 2x6 fascia workpiece in position, allowing excess for end cuts. Project the lines as shown. See Figure 2.

position. Use an adjustable bevel to mark both angles of the compound miters needed for the joints. Check the angles with a protractor, then transfer them to your table saw or radial arm saw.

Check your setup by making the cap for the trellis roof. Cut four pieces of 2x4 stock to form a closed square as shown in the diagram. Once all four pieces are cut, test them on the gazebo itself. It should fit squarely against the bevels on the rafters. If there are gaps, make minor changes in your setup and try again. Attach these four pieces with 16d nails, making sure to predrill the nail holes.

This test avoids wasting valuable lumber while you get the cutting angles exactly right. Once the cap fits properly, you can make the remaining components without changing your settings.

Starting at the lower edge of the roof, cut the trellis members and attach them to the rafters with 16d

Figure 3.
With the fascia board removed, use a bevel gauge to project the center line. This line represents the joint.

galvanized siding nails. It is a good idea to measure each board individually to allow for slight variations in the structure. Bore pilot holes for the nails to prevent splitting the wood. Move up the roof, spacing the trellis boards 15 in. apart.

FINISHING. Finish the shelter by applying two coats of a clear, nontoxic wood sealer and preservative. This finish is best applied with an airless sprayer. Be sure to wear safety glasses and a canister-type respirator.

SAFETY FIRST. Working on an open roof structure like this gazebo is potentially dangerous. For safety's sake, use a 10 ft. or taller stepladder. Stand on an intermediate rung, and avoid overreaching. Rather than lean out to drive a nail or fit a section of the roof, climb down and reposition the ladder.

❖

Figure 4.
Set your circular saw to the correct bevel and cut the fascia at the required angle.

136

Two Projects for the Birds!

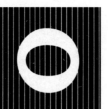

O ur wren house and oriole feeder make great projects for the whole family. Get the older kids involved in cutting out the parts. Even the youngsters can help with fetch-

ing and hammering. While building these projects, you also can teach your children a lot about birds: their habitats, their migration patterns, their feeding habits and even the joy of bird-watching. Your children will enjoy watching the birds come to a house and feeder that they helped build themselves! You may want to make several of these projects at once. They are great for the backyard and make nice Christmas gifts, too.

SKILL LEVEL. Equipped with a saber saw and a power drill, beginning woodworkers will enjoy building these projects and seeing the fruits of their labor quickly and easily. Remember, you don't need to build a fancy birdhouse or feeder to get a bird's attention!

TIPS. Use natural weather-resistant woods like cedar or redwood. Also, avoid using paints, varnishes,

Whether you are partial to wrens, orioles, finches or bluebirds, it is fun and easy to build this enticing home and feeder for your favorite feathered friends.

wood preservatives or any other chemicals to finish the projects. Some of these chemicals may actually keep birds away.

WREN HOUSE. Birds are a natural feature in every garden. You can make the most of these feathered denizens by building attractive nesting boxes. This one, designed for wrens and other small birds, can be hung almost anywhere. Wrens and many other types of birds often nest near human activity centers.

The wren house is built entirely of ½ in. thick cedar. Begin by cutting all of the components from 6 in. wide material.

Start construction by making the two front/back (B) workpieces of the box. Cut the stock to the length shown in the diagram, then lay out the 45 degree angles with a combination square. Cut the parts with a scroll saw. Be careful to make both ends identical.

Next, cut a 45 degree bevel along the entire edge of cedar stock. For safety's sake, always work on a piece of material at least 18 in. long. Then rip the material 5 in. wide. From this material, cut the roof

137

Two Projects for the Birds!

Figure 1.

A combination square is the ideal tool to help you lay out the wren house front/back (B) workpieces. Locate the positions for the perch and the entryway, too.

Figure 2.

Rip a 45 degree bevel into one edge of a length of stock for forming the wren house roof (A), sides (C) and bottom (D). Use a scroll saw and work with material that is at least 18 in. long.

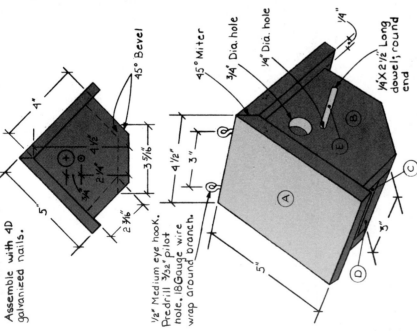

Assemble with 4D galvanized nails.

4"
5"
45° Bevel
3 5/16"
4 1/2"
2 1/4"
3/4"
2 3/16"

1/2" Medium eye hook. Predrill 3/32" pilot hole, 18 Gauge wire wrap around branch.

45° Miter
3/4" Dia. hole
1/4" Dia. hole
4 1/2"
3"
5"
1/4"
1/4" X 2 1/2" Long dowel; round end
1"
A
B
E
C
D

parts (A) to length. Next, cut the bevel for the bottom (D) of the box, and then cut this part to length.

Rip the remaining stock to the 2 3/16 in. width needed for the sides (C) of the box, and cut these parts to their 3 in. finished length.

Bore holes in the front component, as shown in the diagram. Use a backup board to prevent wood splintering.

Assemble the wren house with 4d galvanized finishing nails. Make sure that you predrill the nail holes to avoid splitting the wood.

Add the dowel perch after rounding one end with sandpaper. Attach the dowel using a nontoxic glue such as Titebond II, then drill pilot holes and install

This project is courtesy of Dremel, 4915 21st St., Racine, WI 53406. The tools used include the 16 in. scroll saw (model 1671), disc/belt sander (model 1731), Moto-Tool (model 395) and D-Vise (model 2214).

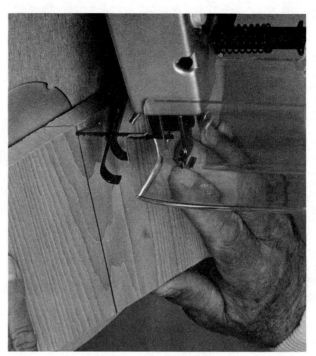

Figure 3.

Here we are cutting the remaining bevel to form the wren house bottom (D). Note that we stop the cut once we are past the proper distance; do not cut along the entire length of the material. Stop the saw and remove the workpiece. Then cut the material to length.

Cutting List

Wren House

A	Roof	½ x 4½ x 5	2
B	Front/back	½ x 4 x 4	2
C	Side	½ x 2³⁄₁₆ x 3	2
D	Bottom	½ x 3 x 3⁵⁄₁₆	1
E	Perch	¼ dia. x 2½	
		hardwood dowel	1

Note: All material is cedar unless otherwise indicated. All dimensions are in inches.

the eye hooks. Be certain that the sharp points of the eye hooks do not extend into the box.

Leave the wren house unfinished. Hang the box in a sheltered location using heavy nylon monofilament fishing line.

ORIOLE FEEDER. The oriole is one of the most colorful birds in North America. Attracting them can add color and pleasure to your outdoor living. This feeder is especially designed to entice orioles with their favorite food: fruit.

Made entirely of cedar, the oriole feeder can be constructed in less than an hour. You can probably build it from materials in your scrap box.

Start by cutting the triangular block for the roof support (CC) from a piece of material at least 6 in. long. Rip the material at a 45 degree angle, then cut to the length shown in the diagram (see next page).

Figure 4.

Use a stationary disk sander with the bed set to 45 degrees. Then finish sand the mitered edges for both the feeder and the birdhouse.

139

Two Projects for the Birds!

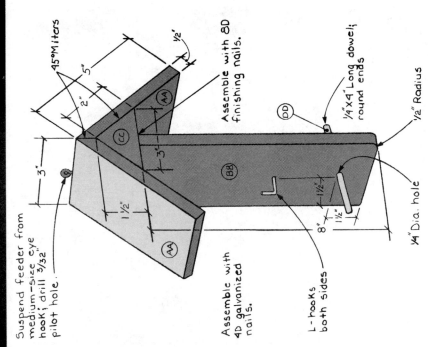

45°Miters

5"

2"

3"

1½"

3"

AA

CC

AA

BB

DD

½"

¼"×4" Long dowel;
round ends

½" Radius

¼" Dia. hole

1½"

1½"

8"

Suspend feeder from
medium-size eye
hook; drill 5/32"
pilot hole.

Assemble with 8D
finishing nails.

Assemble with
4D galvanized
nails.

L-hooks
both sides

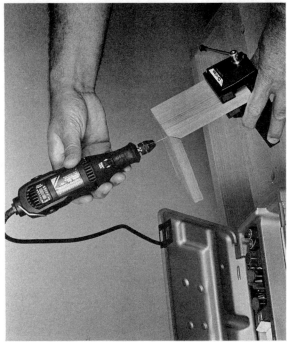

Figure 7.

*Predrill nail holes for attaching the feeder roof (AA) to
the base assembly.*

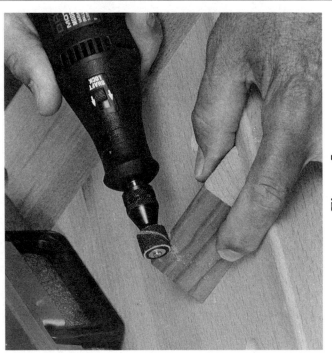

Figure 5.

*Sand two flats in the top of the feeder's triangular roof
support (CC) to allow for nailing. Be sure to predrill the
nail holes.*

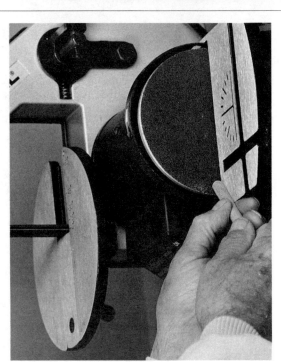

Figure 6.

*Round the edges of the feeder perch (DD) on a disk
sander. Turn the dowel as you apply light pressure against
the sanding disk.*

Next, file two flats in the top of the roof support to allow for nailing. Bore ⅛ in. pilot holes through the block for the nails.

Cut the roof parts (AA) to the size shown in the diagram (on opposite page). You can save time by making both 45 degree miters in one pass.

Also, cut the base (BB) and the perch (DD) to their respective sizes.

Drill a ¼ in. diameter hole in the base to accommodate the perch. Round off the lower corners of the base with a sanding block. Also, round the ends of the dowel, then glue it in place.

Attach the triangular block to the upright with 8d galvanized finishing nails and waterproof glue. Use a nail set to hammer the nails flush with the wood.

Add the roof parts, securing them with 4d galvanized nails and waterproof glue. Install the brass L-hooks as shown in the diagram, then add the eye hook to the roof. For added stability, use two eye hooks.

Leave the feeder unfinished for a rustic look and

to best attract the birds. Hang the feeder in a sheltered location with galvanized wire. Press fruit onto the L-hooks and you will soon have orioles feeding in your yard.

❖

Cutting List

Oriole Feeder

AA	Roof	½ x 3 x 5	2
BB	Base	½ x 3 x 8	1
CC	Roof support	1½ x 3 x 3	1
DD	Perch	¼ dia. x 4 hardwood dowel	1

Note: All material is cedar unless otherwise indicated. All dimensions are in inches.

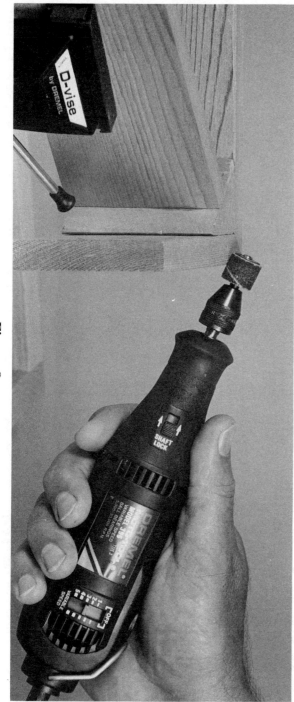

Figure 8.
Dull the edges of the finished project with a drum sander installed in your Moto-Tool. Wear safety goggles and a dust mask.

Hippity-Hoppity Planter

Rabbits and garden plants usually are not a good combination. The rabbits on this whimsical planter, however, will never eat your plants or multiply to fill your yard! Any way you look at it, this is a fun project that will bring you hours of enjoyment and no doubt many compliments upon its completion.

Lots of decisions need to be made about this project. First, get out the flower seed packets and decide which flowers will be the brightest and the bushiest. Next, choose paint colors for the tulips, bunnies and flower box. Should the bunnies be white, gray or two-tone? What color tulips do you prefer?

SKILL LEVEL. This cute project is quite suitable for beginning woodworkers. However, it will provide fun for woodworkers of all ages and all skill levels. The challenging part of the project is choosing and applying paints.

TIPS. All of the project components can be cut out quite safely with the aid of a band saw or saber saw. However, a stationary scroll saw is preferred. It is ideal for cutting small pieces such as the tulips and minimizes the amount of edge-sanding required.

Brighten your yard with this fun and easy-to-build bunny planter. It is a great weekend project!

CONSTRUCTION. We used pressure-treated lumber for the planter's basic frame, but you can substitute cedar or redwood.

Cut out the front/back (A), sides (B) and base (C) on a table saw. Then locate the drainage (or weep) holes in the base. You will need to drill approximately six holes ½ in. in diameter. The holes should be spread evenly in the base, making sure they fall within the area of the planter. Follow up this step by locating and then drilling holes for the 12 tulip stems (F). Again, make sure that these holes will not conflict with the location of the planter and the rabbits (D) when all of the components are installed. Drill the 12 holes into the base to accommodate the ¼ in. diameter stems (F), at a depth of ½ inch.

Use the full-size patterns for the rabbit (D) and the tulip (E) to trace them on plywood. Use graphite paper to transfer the patterns onto the plywood. Make sure that the tulips are cut from wider material to prevent your fingers from getting too close to the blade of the scroll saw. Cut out the tulips and the rabbits on your scroll saw, then smooth the edges of the components with a band sander.

Hippity-Hoppity Planter

Then secure this assembly to the base, using the same fastening techniques.

FINISHING. Finish sand the planter as well as the tulips and the rabbits. Paint the planter, rabbits, tulips and stems using colorful exterior paints. We suggest that you begin by applying a good sealer, lightly sanding once the sealer coat has dried. Then apply one or two coats of exterior paint.

After the paint has dried, attach the two rabbits in place with 3d galvanized finishing nails. Next, glue the tulips to the stems with a resorcinol glue. Finally, glue the stems to the base, and the project is complete!

❖

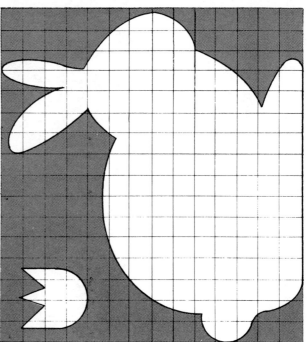

Use spray enamel exterior paints. Sides, base and dowels: green; rabbit: gray. Flower tops: blue, red yellow and orange. (3) Each color.

¼"Dia.X½" deep hole. ½" 1¾" 24"

¼" Dia. dowel vary length from 3" to 6" (12) required.

Drill (6) ½" Dia. weep holes at equal spacing.

Vary spacing ½" to 2½".

4" 5½" 7¼"

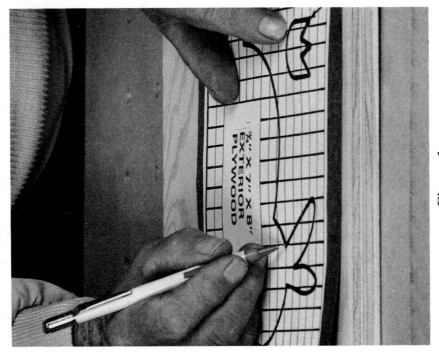

Figure 1.
Trace the pattern for the rabbit (D), then use graphite paper to transfer the pattern onto exterior grade plywood.

Cut ¼ in. diameter hardwood dowels to varying lengths of between 3 to 6 inches. Next, drill ¼ in. diameter by ½ in. deep holes into the base of each of the 12 tulips. Make sure that you securely clamp each tulip to your workbench or in your vise before drilling.

ASSEMBLY. Secure the two sides (B) to the front and back workpieces (A) with 6d galvanized finishing nails and resorcinol (waterproof) glue. Pre-drill the nail holes to prevent the wood from splitting, and drive the nails in at an angle for added strength.

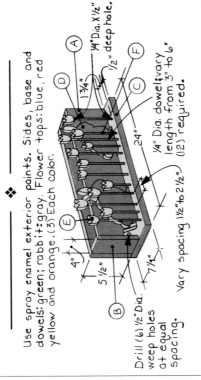

Each Square = ½"

144

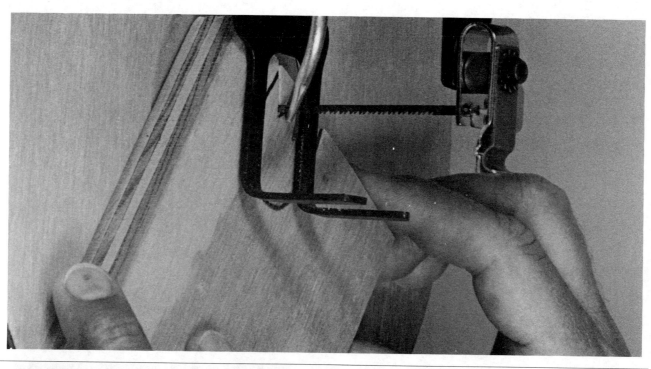

Figure 2.

Lay out the tulip pattern so you have plenty of working space to ensure that your fingers will not get too close to the saw blade. Then cut out the tulip patterns on your scroll saw. As always, make sure you wear safety glasses or goggles to prevent eye injuries.

Cutting List

A	Front/back	3/4 x 5 1/2 x 24	2
B	Side	3/4 x 4 x 5 1/2	2
C	Base	3/4 x 7 1/4 x 24	1
D	Rabbit	3/4 x 7 1/4 x 8	
		exterior plywood	2
E	Tulip	3/4 x 1 1/2 x 1 5/8	
		exterior plywood	12
F	Stem	1/4 dia. x (3-6) dowel	12

Note: All material is pressure-treated unless otherwise indicated. All dimensions are in inches.

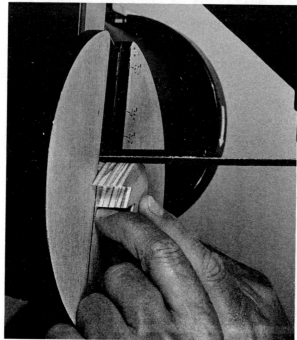

Figure 3.

A band sander is an ideal tool for sanding the edges of both small and large workpieces. Although often over-looked as a basic workshop tool, this simple power tool is invaluable. Most come with guide plates that round inside corners, too.

Kids' Castle

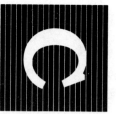

ombine your woodworking skills with your child's imagination and transform your backyard or playroom into a place where Robin Hood and his merry men rescued Maid Marian and where Beauty and the Beast danced and fell in love while a clock and a teapot watched in awe. This play castle is loaded with details that bring fantasies to life — jagged turrets, barred windows, a real drawbridge and even a dungeon! Lower the drawbridge and cross the moat to enter this two-story castle. A ladder leads up to the lookout area, which is complete with flags. Slide back down to ground level, but beware! A vengeful king may imprison your young adventurer in the dungeon below the slide!

SKILL LEVEL. This is a good project for intermediate-level woodworkers. Numerous details require a good understanding of technical drawings.

TIPS. A saber saw and a circular saw are the ideal power tools for cutting out the numerous plywood pieces. It is a good idea to have plenty of saber saw blades on hand before you begin the project, as well as two plywood cutting blades for your circular saw.

Imagine the hours of fun your pint-size kings and queens will have as they pretend in this make-believe castle.

Also, use a straightedge to guide your circular saw along the long cuts. We recommend using APA A-B or A-C exterior-grade plywood. Carefully plan each workpiece's layout before cutting. Where possible, do the layout with the good side down to avoid blemishing the good side when cutting with power tools.

CONSTRUCTION. After carefully laying out each workpiece's design, cut each to its overall shape.

Some of the workpieces, like the shutters (P) and the drawbridge (N), can be cut from the larger blank in which it is installed. For the shutters, this means the side tower fronts (J) and sides (L); for the drawbridge, this means the drawbridge front (K). Do not drill a starter hole with a drill bit to insert the saber saw when cutting the shutters or drawbridge. Instead, make a plunge cut in the design with your saber saw. Make as many plunge cuts as necessary in order to do an accurate job of cutting each silhouette while minimizing wood waste.

Lay out the handle patterns for each of the two ladder sides (X) and also the positioning of the six steps (AA-FF). After locating the handle patterns, drill two 1 in. diameter holes with a Forstner bit and then drill out the section in between

HOW TO CUT THE SHUTTERS

Figure 1.
Some workpieces, like the shutters (P), are laid out on the tower sides (L). Use a bar compass and a straight-edge to lay these out on the nonshowing side. This will reduce wood splintering.

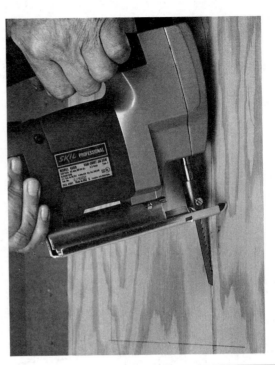

Figure 2.
Cut out the shutters (P) from the tower side (L) by making plunge cuts. Lay the saber saw pad on the plywood and grip the saw as shown. Refer to Figure 3.

with a saber saw. Remember to use a backup board when drilling the holes to eliminate wood splintering.

Next, notch the ends of the inside tower wall workpieces (M). Notice that the longest end of the notch requires a 45 degree cut. Because both workpieces are mirror reflections of one another, they will require that you tilt the pad of your saber saw 45 degrees left of center to make one cut into the workpiece; then tilt the pad of the saber saw 45 degrees right of center to cut the other workpiece. Cut the scrap area with a handsaw.

Lay out and then drill the holes for the flagpole holders (I), the windowsills (Z, OO) and the bar

148

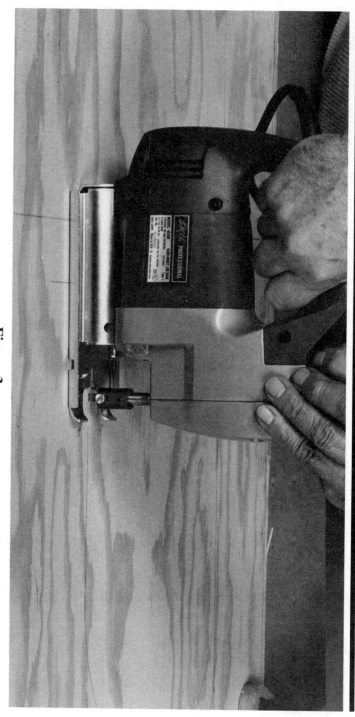

Figure 3.

Complete the plunge cut (see Figure 2) by aligning the saw blade with the cutting line and starting the saber saw. As the saber saw begins cutting through the surface, use only light pressure to move the blade downward until it passes through the plywood. Then stop the saber saw and reposition it for cutting the shutter, as you would normally.

support (VV). Remember to use a backup board when drilling these holes. Note that the size of the hole for the flagpole holders is not stated; that will be determined by the flags you purchase.

It is best to fill in all of the wood blemishes with an appropriate exterior-grade, nontoxic wood filler. Then use a router equipped with a ¼ in. rounding over bit to slightly round all of the plywood edges (with the exception of the edges that will be joined at assembly). This will make the project safer, and it will be easier to accomplish at this phase of construction. Follow this up by finish sanding all of the project parts.

GENERAL ASSEMBLY. Use 4d galvanized finishing nails for joining and 3d finishing nails for attaching workpieces like the shutter stop (Q) and the

drawbridge handle (UU). Also, use a quality exterior-grade nontoxic adhesive for securing all the joints. We found Titebond II wood glue ideal for this application because it will make the project stronger. If you prefer, use No. 10 by 1½ in. brass flathead wood screws for joining and No. 8 by 1¼ in. brass flathead wood screws for attaching workpieces. If you opt to use screws, you will have to predrill all screw holes as well as use glue.

Upper Turret. Begin assembly by putting together the upper turret section. Secure all of the turret workpieces first. These include parts A, B, C, D and E. Then secure the floor supports (H) to the center tower floor (G) and in turn secure this to the turret assembly.

Kids' Castle

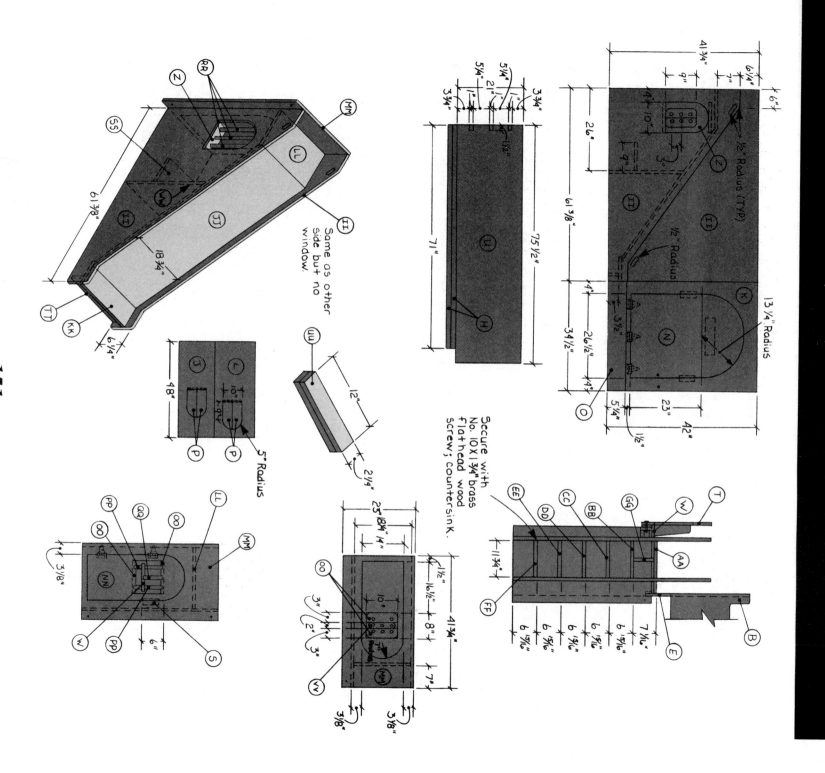

Same as other
side but no
window.

5" Radius

½" Radius (TYP)

½" Radius

13 ¼" Radius

Secure with
No. 10 X 1 ¾" brass
flathead wood
screws; countersink.

151

INSIDE TOWER WALLS

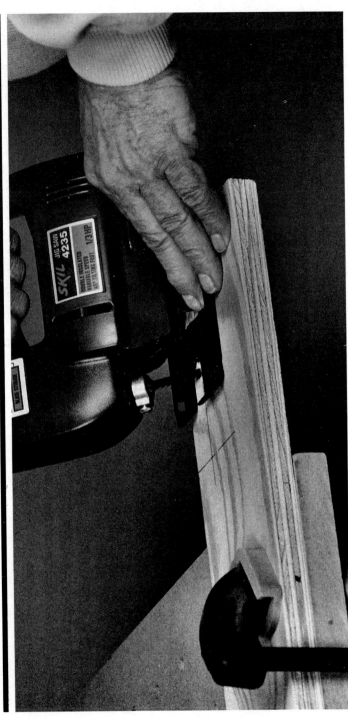

Figure 4.

The two inside tower walls (M) require notches cut at 45 degrees. Each one is a mirror image of the other. To make one cut, readjust the saber saw's pad as shown, 45 degrees left of center, and cut the appropriate inside tower wall. Readjust the saber saw pad so it is 45 degrees right of center to complete the other angled cut.

Now, install the side tower floors (F). Finish the assembly by attaching the four flagpole holders (I).

Lower Castle. Complete the lower portion of the castle by securing the tower sides (L) to the side tower fronts (J). Then attach the inside tower walls (M) and the drawbridge front (K).

Next, add the two shelves (R), the drawbridge entry (O) and the shutter stops (Q). Complete this portion of the assembly by adding the two stops (S) for the drawbridge.

Rear Platform and Ladder. The next phase of assembly entails building the rear platform and ladder.

Figure 5.

Use a handsaw to finish notching the two inside tower walls (M).

Cutting List

		Dimensions	Qty
A	Front side turret	3/4 x 24 x 24 1/4	2
B	Side turret	3/4 x 23 1/2 x 24	2
C	Front center turret	3/4 x 24 x 34 1/2	1
D	Inside front	3/4 x 5 1/4 x 24	2
E	Back side	3/4 x 6 x 30	2
F	Side tower floor	3/4 x 22 x 23 1/2	2
G	Center tower floor	3/4 x 17 1/2 x 65	1
H	Floor support	3/4 x 1 1/2 x 71	2
I	Flagpole holder	3/4 x 2 3/4 x 2 3/4	4
J	Side tower front	3/4 x 18 1/4 x 48	2
K	Drawbridge front	3/4 x 34 1/2 x 42	1
L	Tower side	3/4 x 20 5/8 x 48	2
M	Inside tower wall	3/4 x 6 x 48	2
N	Drawbridge	3/4 x 26 1/2 x 36 1/4	1
O	Drawbridge entry	3/4 x 5 1/4 x 34 1/2	1
P	Shutter	3/4 x 5 x 14	8
Q	Shutter stop	3/4 x 1 x 10	2
R	Shelf	3/4 x 5 x 16 3/4	2
S	Stop	3/4 x 1 1/2 x 6	2
T	Back turret	3/4 x 21 x 60	1
U	Rear floor	3/4 x 21 x 75 1/2	1
V	Turret extension	3/4 x 3 1/2 x 7 3/4	2
W	Turret support	3/4 x 3 1/2 x 11	2
X	Ladder side	3/4 x 8 7/8 x 59 3/4	2
Y	Ladder wall	3/4 x 23 x 41 3/4	1
Z	Windowsill	3/4 x 3 x 9	2
AA	Step	3/4 x 3 3/4 x 11 3/4	1
BB	Step	3/4 x 4 7/16 x 11 3/4	1
CC	Step	3/4 x 5 1/8 x 11 3/4	1
DD	Step	3/4 x 5 13/16 x 11 3/4	1
EE	Step	3/4 x 6 1/2 x 11 3/4	1
FF	Step	3/4 x 7 3/16 x 11 3/4	1
GG	Step support	3/4 x 1 1/2 x 65 5/8	1
HH	Floor support	3/4 x 2 3/4 x 75 1/2	1
II	Slide side	3/4 x 4 13/16 x 61 3/8	2
JJ	Slide	3/4 x 18 3/4 x 52 3/8	1
KK	Slide bottom	3/4 x 18 3/4 x 8	1
LL	Slide top	3/4 x 18 3/4 x 12	1
MM	Dungeon wall	3/4 x 23 x 41 3/4	1
NN	Dungeon door	3/4 x 14 x 31 1/2	1
OO	Windowsill	3/4 x 3 x 10	2
PP	Bar	3/4 dia. x 9 3/4 pine	2
QQ	Bar	3/4 dia. x 6 pine	1
RR	Bar	3/4 dia. x 15 1/2 pine	3
SS	Dungeon seat	3/4 x 9 x 18 3/4	1
TT	Slide front	3/4 x 3 1/2 x 18 3/4	1
UU	Drawbridge handle	3/4 x 2 1/4 x 12	2
VV	Bar support	3/4 x 2 x 8	1
WW	Dungeon wall	3/4 x 18 3/4 x 23 3/4	1

Note: All material is plywood unless otherwise indicated. All dimensions are in inches.

Figure 6.

You can lay out some of the project components, like the turrets (A, B, C), in an interlocking fashion to save on plywood and reduce cutting time.

Begin by securing one of the turret extensions (V) to the rear floor (U). Then add the back turret (T), followed by the remaining turret extension (V).

Now, add the floor supports (H, HH). Finally, add the two turret supports (W) to strengthen the assembly.

It is easier to make the ladder apart from the rear platform at this time.

Secure each of the steps to the ladder sides (X) with glue and No. 10 by 2 in. brass flathead wood

screws. Predrill all the screw holes and countersink the heads. Then secure the step support (GG) in a similar fashion.

To complete the rear platform and ladder, attach the ladder wall (Y) to the rear platform. Secure the ladder assembly by driving either screws or nails through the back of the ladder wall (Y) into the ladder sides (X).

Slide. Carefully lay out the slide pattern on the two slide sides (II). Install the slide top (LL) and then the

154

front (TT).

Add the finishing touches to the dungeon by installing the windowsills (Z, OO), along with the bar support (VV) and dowels (PP, QQ, RR). Glue and nail the dowels in place. Make sure that you predrill all nail holes and use 3d finishing nails.

MAJOR ASSEMBLY AND FINISHING TOUCHES. Add the shutters (P) and dungeon door (NN). Use black or antique-looking strap hinges if possible. If only chrome hinges are available, spray paint them with an appropriate exterior paint. Also, hinge the drawbridge, using at least three heavy-duty hinges.

Finish the door by adding the drawbridge handle (UU), securing it to the door at a level where children can reach it easily. Add a magnetic hinge to the dungeon door installed at the stop (S). Also, make sure that you add *two heavy-duty magnetic hinges* at the stops (S) for keeping the drawbridge upright.

It is best to paint the unit at this time, making sure that everything is covered and will be well protected when left out in the elements. Be sure to apply two or three coats of paint in places where the plywood contacts the ground.

Move the four major castle components to the site of the structure. Make sure that the site is level.

Set the turret section onto the castle, but do not secure it at this time. Position the slide and dungeon assembly in place. Notice that the slide is installed on the right side of the castle as you face the front of the castle. The ladder is on the left back side of the castle. When you are sure that all of the components will fit together well, secure the assembly with appropriately sized brass flathead wood screws.

Lower the drawbridge and install two eye hooks along with chain. To add authenticity to the castle, use veneer bricks around the windows and the dungeon door. Veneer bricks can be purchased from a lumberyard or home center.

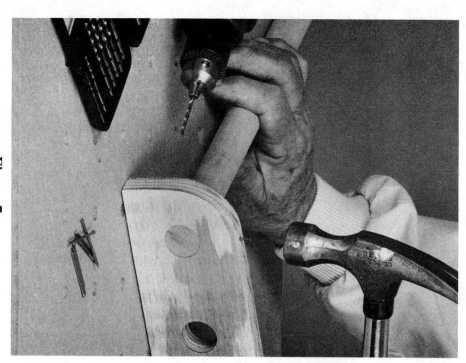

Figure 7.
Drill starter holes for the nails that will secure the bars (PP, QQ) to the windowsills (OO). Drive the finishing nails into the starter holes. It is also a good idea to glue these joints.

Finish the basic assembly by installing the slide bottom (KK). Use an adjustable bevel to determine the angles that the slide (JJ) must be cut. Then attach the slide.

Now, install the two dungeon walls (MM, WW) and the dungeon seat (SS).

This project is courtesy of the American Plywood Association, P.O. Box 11700, Tacoma, WA 98411. How-to photographs are courtesy of Skil Corporation.

Gabled Garden Shed

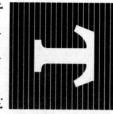

This storage shed will provide you with two things at once: attractive architectural lines to enhance your yard and a practical 80 sq. ft. work and storage space for gardening and landscaping projects. Orient the structure with the main window to the south, and the workbench behind the window becomes the ideal place to get a jump on the gardening season by starting your plants in peat pots.

The shed itself is only 8 ft. by 10 feet. Add the wrap-around deck and it still only needs a space that is 16 ft. by 14 ft. — small enough to allow its gabled roofline to grace all but the smallest of yards.

You'll want to customize the inside to suit your own needs in terms of shelves, workbenches and storage areas for tools or toys. With a little imagination, you can also convert the structure for other uses; you could make it a playhouse, for example, or a poolside cabana.

The shed is designed to be built in sections, so it can be a one-person project with about a half-hour's worth of help from some friends.

We have made every effort to make these plans and instructions easily understandable to the average hobbyist in a home workshop. But words and drawings can only do so much. If you'd like more detailed

Great looks and great work and storage space make this garden shed an ideal project.

explanations and instructions, an instructional videotape showing step-by-step construction is available from the American Plywood Association for $14.95. To order a tape, send a check or money order to APA at P.O. Box 11700, Tacoma, WA 98411. For more information (no orders, please), call (206) 565-6600.

SKILL LEVEL. This shed is suitable for intermediate-level woodworkers who have some construction experience. The construction of the gables presents the greatest challenge.

TIPS. APA trademarked panel products are manufactured in two basic types: panels for permanent exposure to the weather or moisture, and panels for interior use or for protected applications when only temporary exposure to moisture or the weather is required. Within each type are numerous grades — sheathing grades, panels with smooth sanded surfaces on one or both sides, textured panels and panels with overlaid surfaces. Panel recommendations for this project are contained in the Shopping List.

The wood floor and walls can be built inside your shop or garage and carried to the building site by two people. The roof frame can also be carried, though it is heavier. If you don't have enough flat floor space in your shop, the floor of the shed makes a good surface to use for building the walls and roof frame.

Gabled Garden Shed

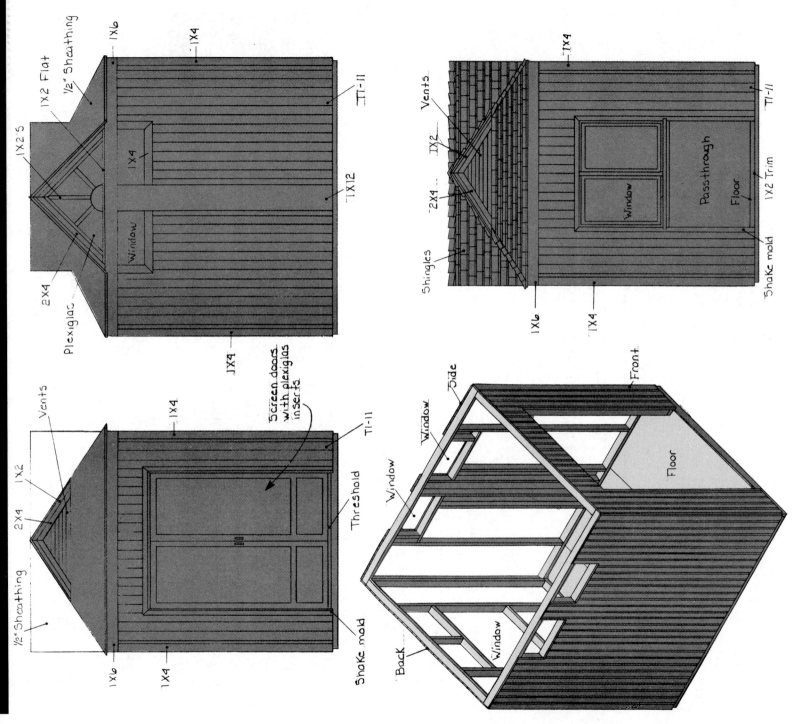

1X2 Flat

½" Sheathing

1X6

1X4

1X2's

1X4

TI-11

Window

1X12

2X4

Plexiglas

1X4

Vents

1X2

2X4

½" Sheathing

1X4

Screen doors with plexiglas inserts

Threshold

TI-11

Shake mold

1X6

1X4

1X4

Vents

1X2

2X4

Shingles

TI-11

Window

1X2 Trim

Passthrough

Floor

Shake mold

1X6

1X4

Window

Side

Window

Front

Floor

Back

Window

Shopping List

Structured Panels

23/32 x 4 ft. x 8 ft. APA rated Sturd-I-Floor	
24 o.c. (tongue & groove) for floor and workbench	3
5/8 x 4 ft. x 8 ft. APA 303 siding (T1-11, 4 in. grooves)	9
1/2 x 4 ft. x 8 ft. APA rated sheathing (CDX or OSB) for roof	5
5/8 x 4 ft. x 8 ft. APA A-C plywood	1
Additional APA panels for shelves	As required

Lumber

2x4 x 8 ft. treated	2
2x4 x 10 ft. treated	7
2x6 x 8 ft. for vent ends	1
2x4 x 8 ft.	46
2x4 x 10 ft.	4
2x4 x 12 ft.	2
2x2 x 8 ft.	4
1 dia. x 4 ft. dowel	2
1/2 x 2 1/2 x 8 ft. trim	7
2 x 8 ft. shake molding	1
1x12 x 8 ft.	2
1x6 x 10 ft.	2
1x6 x 12 ft.	2
1x4 x 8 ft.	10
1x2 x 8 ft.	26
2x4 x 12 ft. cedar	38
2x4 x 10 ft. cedar	6
2x4 x 8 ft. cedar	6
2x8 x 2 ft. cedar	1
3/8 x 3 x 10 ft. cedar benderboards	2
3/8 x 3 x 12 ft. cedar benderboards	4

Other Materials

Gravel, concrete or concrete blocks for foundation	As required
10 in. shelf brackets (more for optional shelves)	16
30 x 96 plastic laminate for workbench top	1
3 in. hinges	2 pairs
2 in. knobs	2
Screen, 30 x 36	1
Pre-hung window, 48 x 36	1
Pre-hung double screen doors, 8 x 5 ft. x 6 ft.	1
Roofing material	2 squares
1/8 x 30 x 60 acrylic for sunburst windows	2
1/8 x 12 x 24 acrylic for side windows	4
2 x 12 framing straps & nails	8
Nails and screws (16d galvanized box for framing; 8d galvanized box for siding, floor and trim; 6d galvanized or bright box for roof sheathing; 5d galvanized finish for window stops; 16d galvanized finish for cedar decking); paint or stain.	

Note: All material is standard construction grade
lumber unless otherwise indicated.

This project is courtesy of the American Plywood Associa-
tion, P.O. Box 11700, Tacoma, WA 98411.

Building Hints

These general hints will help you achieve the best possible results in working with plywood.

Planning. Before starting, study the plan carefully to make sure you understand all of the details.

Making Layout. Following the panel layout, draw all of the parts on the panel using a straightedge and a carpenter's square for accuracy. Use a compass to draw corner radii. Be sure to check the width of your saw cut and allow for saw kerfs when plotting the dimensions.

Cutting. When handsawing, support the panel firmly with the best side facing up. Use a 10 to 15 pt. crosscut saw. Use a fine-tooth coping saw for curves. For inside cuts, start the hole with a drill and use a coping or keyhole saw. When power sawing on a table saw, the best side of the panel should be faceup. A plywood cutting blade gives excellent results, but a sharp combination blade may also be used. When using a portable power saw, the best side of the panel should be facedown. For curved cuts, use a saber saw. Be sure the blade enters the face of the panel. Use the finest tooth possible for a smooth and even cut. For prolonged cutting of nonveneer panels and those containing layers of reconstituted wood, a carbide-tipped blade is suggested.

Make your first cuts to reduce the panel to pieces small enough for easy handling. Plan to cut matching parts with the same saw setting. Scrap lumber clamped or tacked securely in place beneath the panel prevents the workpiece from splintering on the back side.

Overlaid panels can be worked in the same manner as regular grades, with these notable exceptions: sawing and drilling should always be done with the cutting edge of the tool entering the panel face. To minimize chipping at the point of tool exit, use a piece of scrap wood as a backup or place tape along the line of the cut.

Drilling. Support the panel firmly. Use a bit for larger holes and a brace. When the point of the tool appears through the panel, reverse the panel and complete the hole from the back. Finish slowly to avoid splintering the wood.

Planing. Remember, the edge grain of the panel runs in alternate directions, so plane from the ends toward the center. Set the blade for a shallow cut.

Sanding. Many APA panels are sanded smooth in manufacture — one of the big time-savers in their use — so only minimum surface sanding is necessary. After sealing, use fine sandpaper and sand in the direction of the grain only. You may find it easier to sand the cut edges smooth before assembling each unit. Use a medium or finer sandpaper before the sealer or flat undercoat is applied.

Assembly. Constructing the project by section makes the final assembly easier. Drawers, cabinet shells and compartments, for example, should be handled as individual units. For the strongest possible joints, use glue with screws or nails. Check for a good fit by holding all of the pieces together. Contact should be made at all points for lasting strength. Mark the nail locations along the edge of the piece to be nailed. In careful work where nails must be very close to an edge, predrill using a drill bit slightly smaller than the nail size. Always predrill for screws.

Apply glue to clean surfaces in accordance with the manufacturer's instructions. Press the surfaces firmly together until a bead of glue appears. Check for square, then nail and apply clamps if possible to maintain pressure until the glue sets. For exterior exposure, use resorcinol (waterproof) glue; for interior work use liquid resin (white) or urea resin glues. Other glues are available for special gluing applications.

Finishing for Interior Use. Little, if any, surface preparation is usually required. Sanded panels need only light sanding to remove blemishes or to raise grain. If an opaque finish is to be used, cover any knots, pitch streaks or sap spots with shellac or a stain-resistant sealer. Do not apply finishes over dust, glue or spots of oil.

Three types of finishes may be used for interior applications: paints, stains and natural finishes.

When using paints, a solvent-thinned (oil-based) primer should be used to minimize grain raise and prevent staining. Gloss and semi-gloss enamel top coats provide a washable, durable surface. The top coat may be oil-based or alkyd-based (solvent-thinned) or latex (water-thinned), provided it is compatible with the primer.

Panels intended for natural finishes should be carefully selected for pattern and appearance. For the most natural appearance, use two coats of a clear finish, such as a urethane, varnish or clear sealer. To pleasantly subdue any grain irregularities or repairs, a light stain may be applied either by color toning, which uses companion stain and nonpenetrating sealer, or by light staining, which uses a pigmented sealer, tinting material (stain, thin enamel or undercoat) and finish coat (varnish or lacquer). Finish Medium Density Overlaid panels with a solid-color acrylic latex stain or a two-coat paint system (primer plus companion top coat).

Finishing for Exterior Use. A top-quality stain or paint will help maintain the panel's appearance and protect it from weathering. Because end grain absorbs and loses moisture rapidly, panels should be edge-sealed to help minimize possible damage. Use paint primer to seal panels that will be painted, or use a paintable water-repellent preservative for panels that are to be stained.

For rough or textured panels, high-quality stain or acrylic house paints are recommended. Use a solvent-thinned, semitransparent stain for maximum grain show-through. Use an acrylic latex solid-color stain when you want to hide the grain and color (but not the texture) of the wood's surface. Maximum protection of the wood is obtained by using a house paint that consists of a stain-resistant primer and one or more acrylic latex top coats. Finish Medium Density Overlaid panels with solid-color acrylic latex stain or a two-coat paint system (primer plus companion top coat).

Best performance is achieved by applying the first coat of finish with a brush. If the first coat of finish is sprayed on, it should be back-brushed or back-rolled to work it well into the wood's surface. Additional coats may be sprayed without back-brushing.

Whatever finishing method is used — paint or stain — always use top-quality materials and follow the manufacturer's instructions. ❖

Gabled Garden Shed

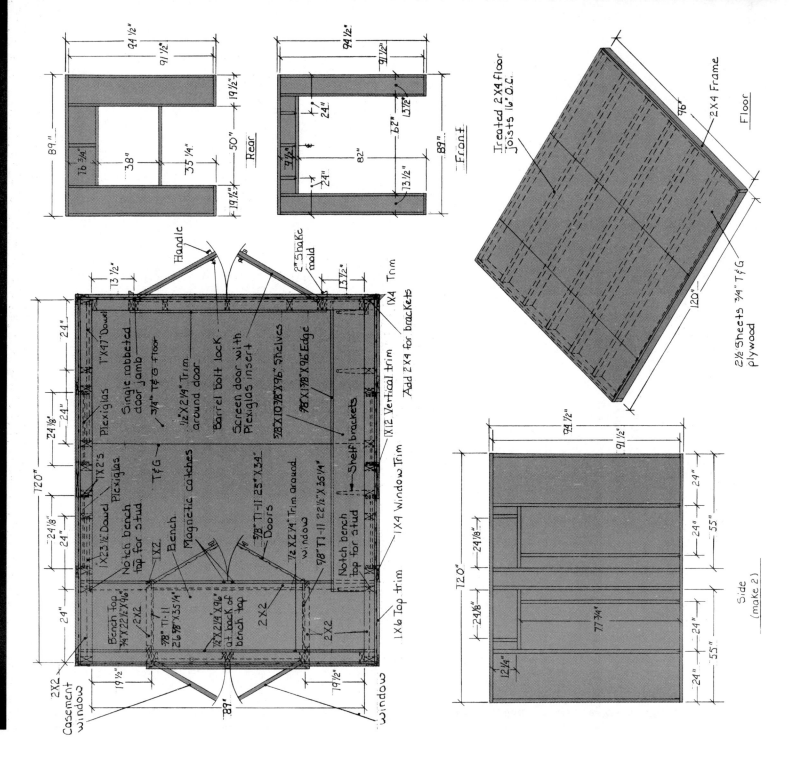

Rear

94½"
91½"
89"
19½"
16¾"
38"
35¼"
50"
19½"

Front

94½"
91½"
89"
24"
82"
24"
13½"
15½"
9½"
24"

Treated 2X4 floor
Joists 16" O.C.
2X4 Frame
Floor
96"
120"
2½ Sheets ¾" T&G
plywood

Handle
2" Shake mold
13½"
15½"
1X4 Trim
Add 2X4 for brackets
Plexiglas   1X47" Dowel
Single rabbeted door jamb
¾" T&G floor
½"X2¼" Trim around door
Barrel bolt lock
Screen door with Plexiglas insert
⅝"X10⅞"X96" Shelves
⅝"X10⅞"X96" Edge
Shelf brackets
1X12 Vertical trim
1X4 Window Trim
1X2's
T&G
Magnetic catches
⅝" T1-11 25"X34"
Doors
½"X2¼" Trim around window
⅝" T1-11 22½"X35¼"
Notch bench top for stud
Bench Top ¾"X22½"X96"
2X2
⅝" T1-11 26⅞"X35¼"
½"X2¼"X96" at back of bench top
2X2
2X2
Bench
Notch bench top for stud
1X2¾ Dowel
Notch bench top for stud
Plexiglas
1X6 Top trim
2X2
Casement window
19½"
24"
24"
24⅛"
24"
120"
24⅛"
24"
73½"
24"
89"
19½"
Window

Side (make 2)
94½"
91½"
120"
24⅛"
24⅛"
24"
24"
55"
24"
24"
55"
12¼"
77¾"

162

When selecting panels for your application, always look for the APA trademark. The mark signifies that the manufacturer is committed to APA's rigorous program of quality supervision and testing and that panel quality is subject to verification through APA audit.

Many other exciting plans are available from the American Plywood Association. To receive a complete listing of indoor and outdoor furniture, storage and recreation projects, write the American Plywood Association, P.O. Box 11700, Tacoma, WA 98411. Enclose $2 to cover postage and handling.

SAFETY FIRST. Remember that safety is more than slogans and signs. A project is no fun if you injure yourself. Years of potential enjoyment will be lost if each time you look at the shed you remember how much it hurt. Follow tool manufacturers' recommendations and use caution and common sense around electricity and cutting tools. The most important safety item in any workshop is safety glasses; splinters that rate some iodine and a bandage on your finger can cost you your sight if they wind up in your eye.

CONSTRUCTION. Select and level the site for the gabled shed. A leveled-gravel foundation is the simplest, and is therefore recommended. Simply dig out 3 in. of soil, replace it with gravel and level. Other options are a concrete slab or concrete blocks.

If you live in an area where high winds are possible, you will want to anchor the structure in accordance with local procedures and guidelines.

Floor and Wall Construction. Construct the floor frame using treated 2x4 lumber. Nail the floor panels over the frame. Ensure that the long dimension runs perpendicular to the joists. Do not push the tongue and groove edges completely together; leave a ⅛ in. space so the panels can expand without causing buckling.

Study the framing guides for the walls, then build the frames on a flat surface, such as your workshop floor. Nail on the siding after cutting out spaces for windows and doors. Be sure to buy your pre-hung doors and windows before framing and cutting out the siding. If you find a bargain in something slightly off-size, it is easy to make adjustments before building the wall section.

If the shed floor is to be used for building the roof frame, set the walls aside for now. To erect walls, set one side in place and temporarily brace it with diagonal 2x4s. Nail to the floor with 16d nails, angled so they penetrate the outboard joist. Then set the back wall and the other side wall in place, nailing to the floor and to each other. Set the front wall in last, nailing to the floor and sides.

Roof Construction. There are plenty of chances to make mistakes when building this structure, so go slowly. Read the plans carefully and think about how the sheathing is going to overlay the structure.

Step 1. Construct the roof frame using two 121½ in. 2x4s and four 94 in. 2x4s. Be sure that no large knots occur where the frame, valleys and rafters come together. You will have to drive several nails close together, and you will need to make sure that the wood remains structurally sound.

The framing straps are typically bought flat. Install them by nailing one side, then bending while tapping with the hammer for a firm fit. Now, nail the other side. Use strapping nails that do not penetrate all of the way through the lumber.

Step 2. Install the end rafters (A). Place the *fish mouth* lower ends in position; nail the top and then nail the bottom to the frame.

Step 3. Nail the main ridge (61 in.) between two sets of end rafters. Note how the ridge is positioned vertically so that the top edge of the ridge meets the top edge of the rafters.

Step 4. Install the gable end rafters (B) and the ridges (46½ in. 2x4s).

Step 5. Install the valleys (C). At both ends, the top side of the valley should touch the top side of the ridges or rafters.

Gabled Garden Shed

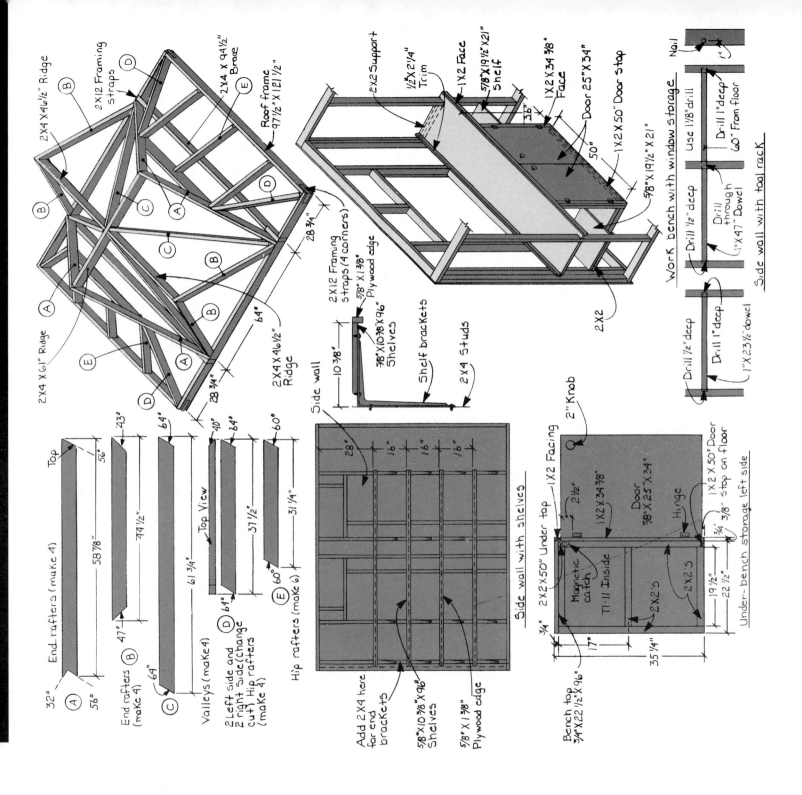

2X4 X4½" Ridge Ⓑ

2X12 Framing Straps

Ⓓ

2X4X4½" Brace

Ⓔ

Roof frame 97½"X 121½"

2X4 X 61" Ridge Ⓐ

28¾"

64"

Ⓔ

2X4X46½" Ridge

28¾"

End rafters (make 4)

Ⓐ 32° 56°

Top

Ⓑ 23°

End rafters (make 4)

47°

64°

Ⓒ 64°

74½"

58⅞"

61¾"

Top View

40°

64°

31½"

Ⓓ 2 Left side and 2 right side (change cut) Hip rafters (make 4)

Valleys (make4)

60°

60°

31¼"

Ⓔ Hip rafters (make 6)

2X12 Framing straps(4 corners)

5/8" X 1 3/8" Plywood edge

Side wall

10 3/8"

5/8"X10 3/8"X96" Shelves

Shelf brackets

2X4 Studs

Add 2X4 here for end brackets

5/8"X10 3/8"X 96" Shelves

5/8" X 1 3/8" Plywood edge

2.8"   16"   16"   16"

Side wall with shelves

2X2 Support

½"X2¼" Trim

1X2 Face

5/8"X19½"X21" Shelf

Drill ½" deep

16"

Door 25"X34"

1X2X34 3/8" Face

50"

1X2X50" Door stop

5/8"X 19½"X 21"

2X2

Work bench with window storage

Nail

1"

Use 1/8" drill

Drill 1" deep 60" From floor

Side wall with tool rack

Drill 1/8" drill

Drill through 1"X47" Dowel

Drill ½" deep

Drill 1" deep

1"X23½" dowel

Drill ½" deep

2" Knob

3/4"   2X2X50" Under top

1X2 Facing

Magnetic catch

2½"

1X2 X 34 3/8"

Door 5/8"X25"X34"

1X2 X 50" Door stop on floor

Hinge

3/8" stop on floor

¾"

T1-11 Inside

2X25

2X25

19½"

22½"

35¼"

17"

¾"

Bench top ¾"X22½"X96"

Side wall with shelves

Under-bench storage left side

164

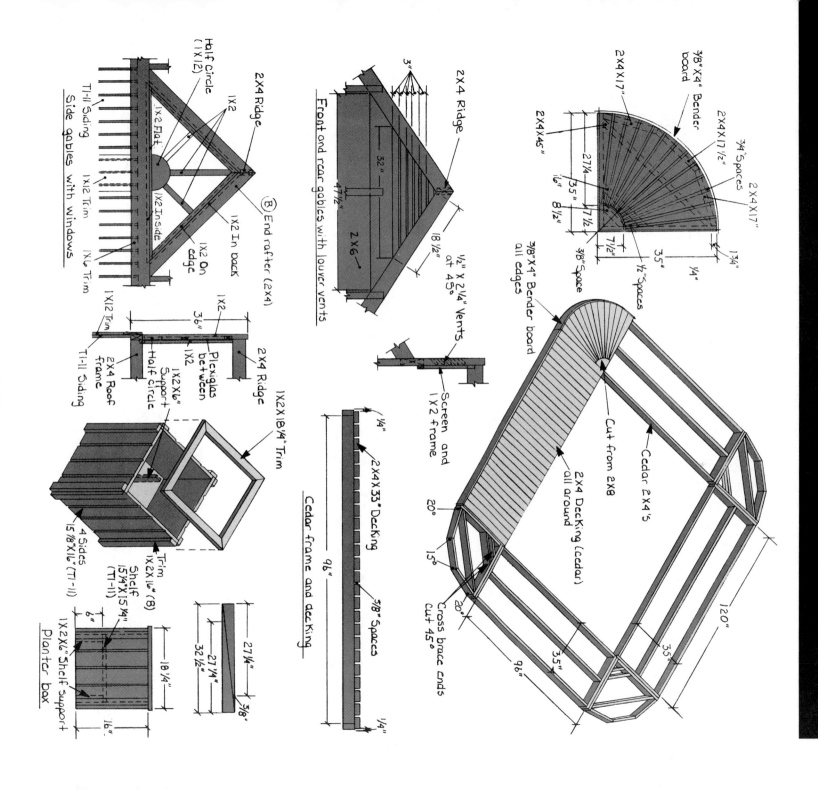

Side gables with windows

Half circle (1X12)

1X2

2X4 Ridge

Ti-11 Siding
1X12 Trim
1X6 Trim

1X2 Flat

1X2 Inside

1X2 In back

1X2 On edge

Ⓑ End rafter (2x4)

Front and rear gables with louver vents

2X4 Ridge

3"

32"

47½"

18½"

2x6

½" x 2¼" Vents at 45°

Screen and 1X2 frame

1X12 Trim
Ti-11 Siding

2X4 Roof frame

1X2
36"
1X2
Plexiglas between
1X2
1X2X6" Support Half circle

2X4 Ridge

1X2X18¼" Trim

Cedar frame and decking

¼"

2X4X33" Decking

96"

⅝" Spaces

¼"

27¼"
32½"
⅜"

Trim 1X2X16" (8)
4 Sides 15⅞"X16" (TI-11)

Shelf 15¾"X15¼" (TI-11)

6"
18¼"
16"

1X2X6" Shelf support
Planter box

3/8"X4" Bender board

2X4X17"

¾" Spaces
2X4X17½"
2X4X17"

2X4X45"

27¼"
35"
16"
7½"
8½"
½" Spaces
¼"
7½"
13¾"
¼"
35"
3/8" Space

3/8"X4" Bender board all edges

3/8"X4" Bender board all edges

Cedar 2X4's

Cut from 2X8

2X4 Decking (cedar) all around

20°
15°
20°
20°

Cross brace ends cut 45°

120"
96"
35"
35"

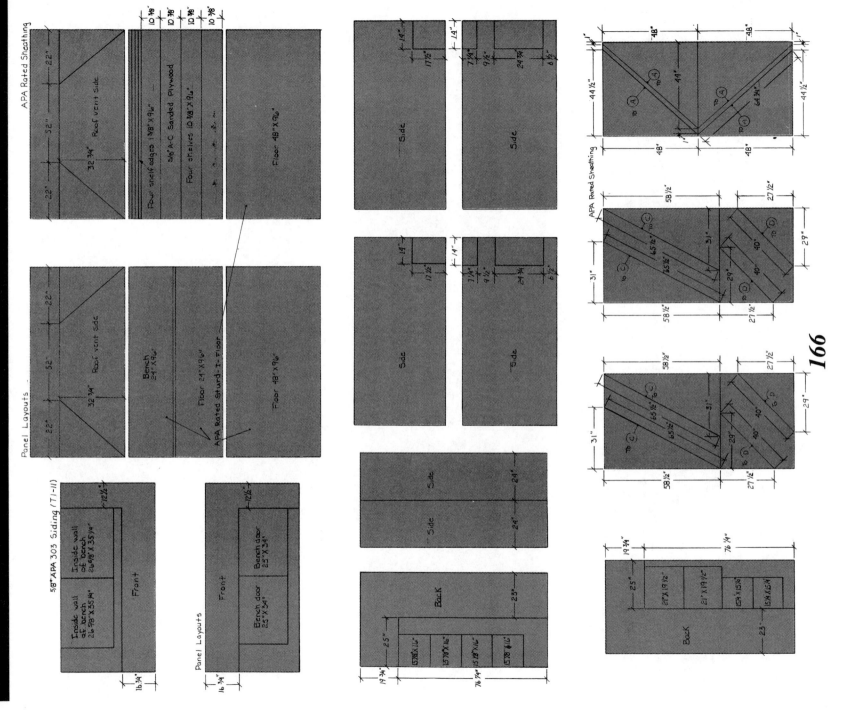

APA Rated Sheathing

22"
52"
22"
32 3/4"
Roof vent side

Panel Layouts

22"
52"
22"
32 3/4"
Roof vent side

10 7/8"
10 7/8"
10 7/8"
10 7/8"
Four unch edges 1 7/8" X 9 1/6"
5/8" A-C Sanded Plywood
Four shelves 10 7/8" X 9 1/6"

Floor 48" X 9 1/6"

Bench 24" X 9 1/6"
Floor 24" X 9 1/6"
APA Rated Sturd-I-Floor

Floor 48" X 9 1/6"

5/8" APA 303 Siding (T1-11)
Inside wall of bench 26 5/8" X 35 1/4"
Inside wall of bench 26 5/8" X 35 1/4"
Front
12 1/2"
16 3/4"

Panel Layouts
Front
Bench door 25" X 34"
Bench door 25" X 34"
12 1/2"
16 3/4"

14"
17 1/2"
Side

14"
7 1/4"
9 1/2"
24 3/4"
6 1/2"
Side

14"
17 1/2"
Side

14"
7 1/4"
9 1/2"
24 3/4"
6 1/2"
Side

Side
Side
24"
24"

2.5"
Back
23"
19 3/4"
15 7/8" X 11"
15 7/8" X 11"
15 7/8" X 11"
15 7/8" X 11"
76 3/4"

1"
48"
48"
1"
44 1/2"
44"
to A
A
to A
A
64 3/4"
44 1/2"
48"
48"

APA Rated Sheathing
58 1/2"
27 1/2"
31"
65 1/2"
65 1/2"
31"
to C
C
29"
40"
40"
to D
D
29"
to C
to D
58 1/2"
27 1/2"

58 1/2"
27 1/2"
31"
65 1/2"
65 1/2"
31"
to C
C
29"
40"
40"
to D
D
29"
to C
to D
58 1/2"
27 1/2"

19 3/4"
76 1/4"
25"
21" X 19 1/2"
21" X 19 1/2"
15 1/4" X 15 1/4"
15 1/4" X 15 1/4"
Back
23"

166

Step 6. Attach 2x6 vent supports (47½ in.) to the end rafters.

Step 7. Install the hip ridge rafters (D). To make compound miters, scribe a line at 64 degrees and set your saw blade at 40 degrees. Four rafters are required; two are mirror images of the other two.

Install each rafter with the bottom end raised above the inside of the frame, so that the sheathing will lay flat on the rafter and the outboard edge of the frame. Install the hip rafters (E) the same way.

Step 8. Install the vent louvers. Make them of ½ in. by 2¼ in. lumber, or use bullnose molding for an extra-finished appearance. Cut the ends at 45 degrees, which will give the louvered angle. Nail from the back, starting at the bottom. Staple the screen from behind. The frame may be installed now, or you can wait until installing the other trim.

Step 9. Measure, cut and fit the roof sheathing, but do not nail it in place.

Step 10. Gather three or more friends, half of them with stepladders, and hoist the roof to the top of the walls. Nail it in place, nail the sheathing on and then finish the roof with flashing and shingles or other roofing material.

Doors, Windows, Shelves and Trim. These may be installed in order of preference, with one exception. If a window is selected with hardware that protrudes into the interior, the shelf underneath the window should be installed before the window. The configuration of the shelf requires that it be installed by placing one end in position while holding the other end up, then sliding the upper end down over the 2x4 stud. Protruding window hardware would prevent this procedure.

To install the acrylic (Plexiglas) windows, first build the frame of 1x2s behind the end rafters. Set the acrylic in caulking and then install the outside frame of 1x2s on edge. Finally, install the decorative sunburst window.

If the trim is to be painted a different color than the siding, you may prefer to paint the trim before installing it, especially the trim around the windows.

Deck Construction. Build the deck of cedar, treated lumber or other wood that weathers well.

For the straight sides, after the frame is constructed, begin nailing the deck pieces by nailing the end pieces in place, ¼ in. back from the end of the frame. Starting at one end, use a ⅝ in. block to position each deck piece, tacking them in place. If the gap at the other end is too large or too small, go back and adjust the other pieces until the gap differences are not noticeable. Nail the decking down with nonstaining finish nails.

For the corner pieces, build the 2x4 frame, then mount the quarter-circle 2x8 one-quarter in. from the frame edges. Nail the two outside beveled decking pieces first, leaving ¼ in. at the edge. Next, measure to the center and mount the center decking piece. Then arrange the five pieces between one side and the center so the gaps are even. Repeat this process for the other corners.

Install benderboards flush with the top of the decking. For corners, use clear, straight-grain wood, longer than needed. Nail one end, and bend around, nailing as you go. Cut off the excess. For an extra-finished appearance, round the outside edges of the 2x4 decking with a belt sander to match the benderboard radius.

Finishing Touches. Use the siding left over from the window cutouts to construct the planter, and paint the plywood and trim to match the colors of the shed. For details on paint/stain selection, see the Building Hints sidebar.

❖

SPECIAL TOOL SECTION: SABER SAWS

SKIL

JIG SAW 4395

169

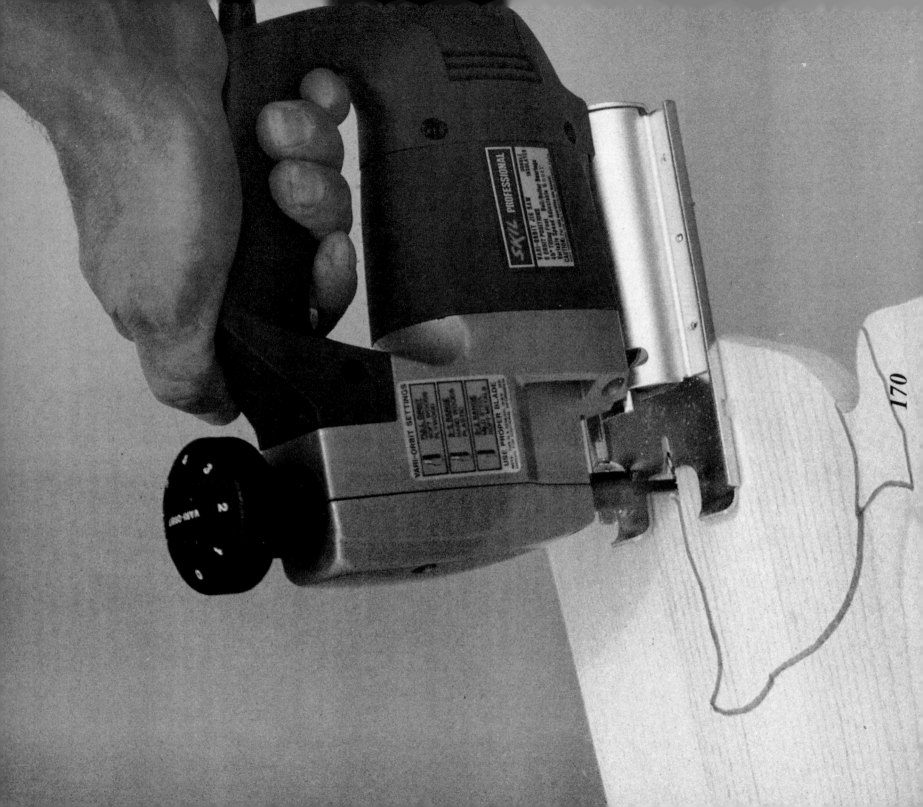

Saber Saw Basics

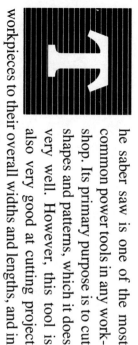

The saber saw is one of the most common power tools in any workshop. Its primary purpose is to cut shapes and patterns, which it does very well. However, this tool is also very good at cutting project workpieces to their overall widths and lengths, and in some cases to their final size.

Our special Basics section will show you how to use the saber saw properly, how to maximize its capabilities and what to look for when buying a saber saw. With virtually hundreds of saber saws on the market, buying the right tool can be difficult.

NOMENCLATURE.

The saber saw is also called a scrolling jigsaw or a jigsaw. Either term is correct, although scrolling jigsaws have the added feature of a saw assembly that can rotate 360 degrees. We will discuss this feature later.

BASIC FEATURES.

All saber saws have a blade that moves up and down and an adjustable pad. All of them allow you to rip, miter and cut designs. However, there are a variety of other features that you can get when you purchase a saber saw. Some of the new tools on the market are cordless, have variable-speed controls, include orbital action, or

Also known as a jigsaw, this relatively inexpensive tool is a must in any home workshop.

have scrolling heads that allow the blade to rotate 360 degrees.

Stroke. The total distance that a blade moves from where it peaks upward and downward is referred to as its cutting stroke. You may be surprised to know that saber saws vary from tool to tool when determining the stroke. Generally, consumer tools have shorter strokes (5/8 in.) than professional tools (13/16 inch).

A longer stroke translates into faster cutting, because more of the blade is coming into contact with the wood. Faster cutting also keeps the blade sharper for a longer period of time. When possible, pay the extra money for a tool with a longer stroke.

Ripping and Crosscutting.

All saber saws allow you to rip materials to length (crosscut) and width (rip). Usually, the resulting edge of each cut is less than desirable for most applications, because the edges still must be jointed or sanded.

The type of blade you use can diminish the roughness of the edges. The more teeth the blade has, the smoother the cut. For instance, a plywood cutting blade will minimize wood splintering and make a smoother cut than a blade with fewer teeth.

The width of the blade also makes a big difference. Narrower blades tend to weave more than wider

171

BLADES FOR TIGHT SPOTS

Shown are three typical saber saw blade sizes. The wider 1 in. blade on the left provides straight cuts (8 tpi). The middle 1/4 in. blade is good for all around ripping, crosscutting and scroll work (8 tpi). The 1/8 in. blade on the right offers smooth, intricate cutting for tight curves (12 tpi).

Figure 1.
Drill a starter hole near the point where you want to begin cutting. If the hole to be cut is square, you may want to make more than one starter hole.

blades. Obviously, narrower blades are ideal for cutting tight curves, but wider blades are preferred for long, slow-curving cuts.

To produce straighter cuts, use a wider blade and a clamped straightedge to guide the saber saw. For smoother crosscuts, use a straightedge as well.

Mitering. The saber saw's foot or pad can be set to swivel left and right of center, usually by 45 degrees. This ability lets you rip or crosscut bevels in woods. Again, the use of a wider plywood cutting blade provides a smoother, straighter cut. Guide the tool against a clamped straightedge.

Unfortunately, the angle calibrations on many tools are not precise. Use a small protractor to give

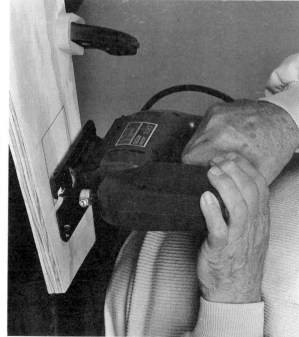

Figure 2.
Insert the saber saw and begin cutting the design pattern.

173

PLUNGE CUTTING

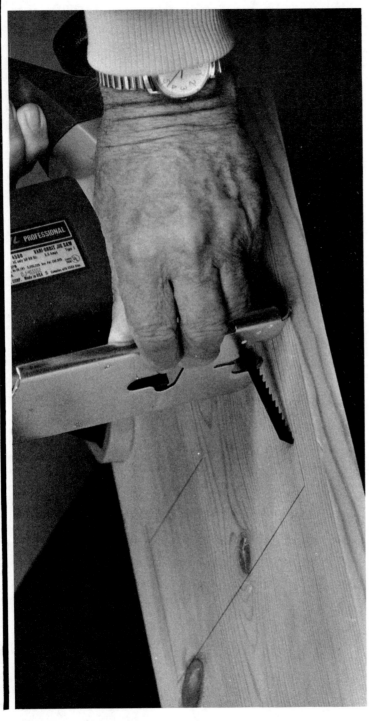

Figure 3.

Begin by holding the tool firmly, so the blade is aligned with the cutting line. Make sure to wear adequate eye protection.

you more precise angle-setting calibrations, and make test cuts before you cut the good material.

Cutting Patterns. This is what the saber saw does best. However, most of us make the mistake of using an old blade to make these cuts. For a rough cut, the old blade is fine. To aim for a perfect cut, install a brand-new blade, one that is suitable for the type of cut you want, and let the tool do the cutting. Never push the tool hard into the wood or turn the blade hard into the cut — both will result in a rough cut and may even bend the blade. If the blade bends, it will begin cutting at an angle. When this happens in the middle of a cut, backing out the blade and cutting again may

Figure 4.

Turn on the saber saw and move the cutting blade down into the material. Apply only light pressure.

174

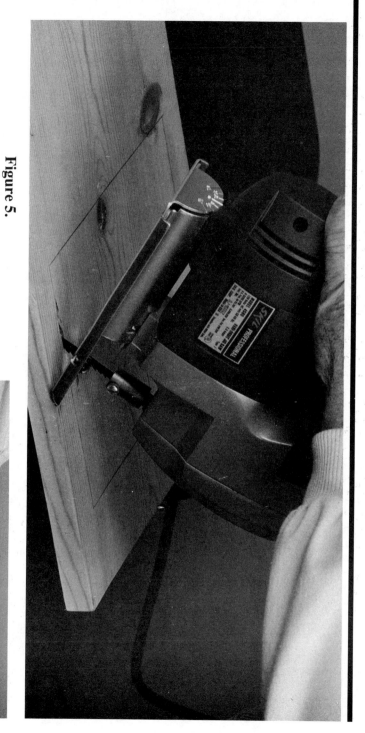

Figure 5.
The front of the pad remains stationary while you pivot the cutting saber saw down into the wood.

not square the cut, even though the blade may not be permanently bent.

Pushing too hard heats up the blade and will cause the blade to bend or to wear out prematurely.

Excessive pushing can be felt and heard. You will not be able get the tool to move appreciably faster with excessive pushing, and you will hear the tool's motor labor more.

Scrolling. A saber saw with a scrolling feature means that the saw blade assembly can be rotated, usually 360 degrees. A lock keeps the blade assembly from moving during a cut. For cuts in a variety of directions, the assembly can be unlocked so that you determine the direction of the cut. This feature allows you to make intricate, curved cuts. Most manufacturers allow the blade to be locked at 90 degree settings.

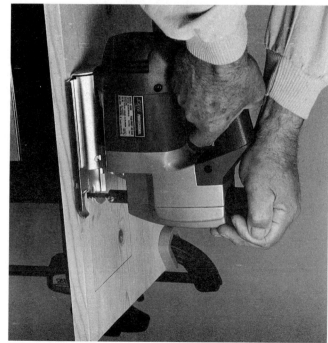

Figure 6.
When the blade breaks through the wood, stop the saber saw. Then finish the cut as you normally would.

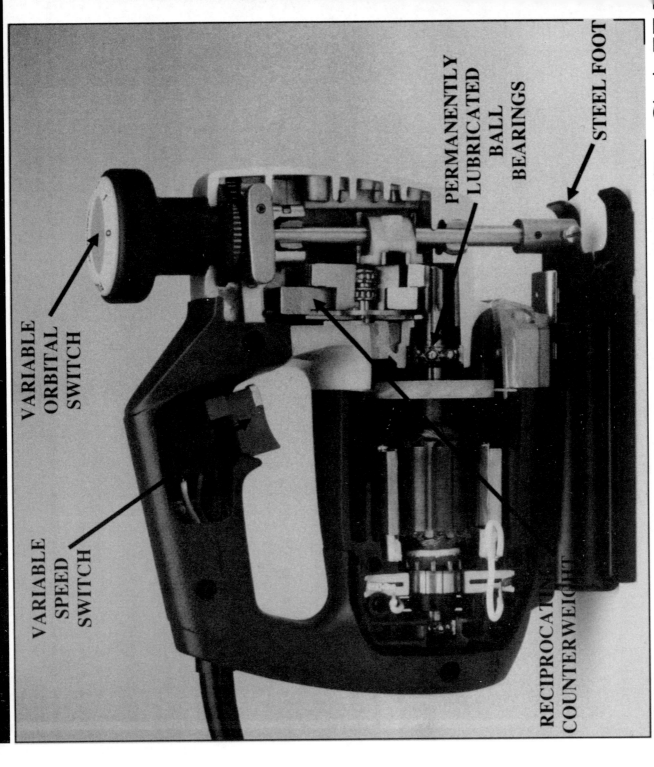

VARIABLE
ORBITAL
SWITCH

VARIABLE
SPEED
SWITCH

PERMANENTLY
LUBRICATED
BALL
BEARINGS

STEEL FOOT

RECIPROCATING
COUNTERWEIGHT

MAKINGS OF A SABER SAW

Here are the basic components of a professional-grade saber saw. This particular tool offers reciprocating action, an electronic variable-speed control and a scrolling feature.

176

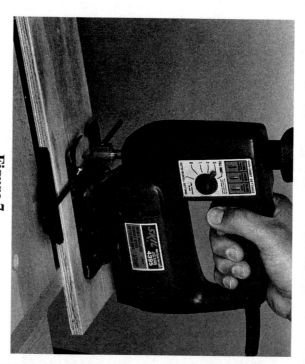

Figure 7.
An adjustable guide is very handy for ripping narrow material. Use a wide blade for ripping.

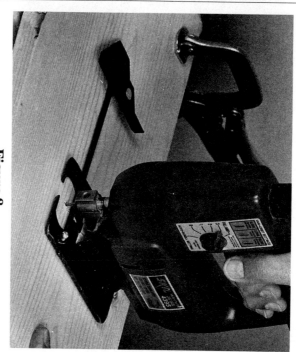

Figure 8.
Some ripping guides can be adapted to cut a circle. Place the pivot end on the wood and make the cut as shown. Notice that a starter hole or plunge cut needs to be made first.

Sometimes a cut results in the saw's pad being off the edge. In these situations the pad may not give you firm tool control. Therefore, by setting the scroll assembly 180 degrees, the pad can rest firmly on the material while you cut, backing up the saw.

Cordless. A cordless saber saw is invaluable for many situations. The short-term energy source (battery) does not really make the cordless saber saw enticing. It is ideal for short-term cutting, but the tool does not have enough battery power for jobs that require more than 15 minutes of continuous cutting. The cordless saber saw is appropriate for cutting a vent opening at home or at a cottage where power is not available. As a staple of the workshop, however, the cordless saber saw may be a disappointing addition.

Speed. Speed is rated as strokes per minute. The more strokes per minute, the faster the tool cuts. This

may be fine in wood but not in metal. When cutting metal, the tool works best at a slower stroke. This rationale is applied to cutting other material types. A single-speed saber saw will suit most workshop purposes.

If you seek more cutting control, variable-speed tools are available that can be set to cut from between 0 to 3,200 strokes per minute.

Speed also must take into account the tool's length of stroke. A tool with a higher number of strokes per minute and a shorter stroke may cut slower than a tool with fewer strokes per minute but a longer stroke.

To compare the real cutting ability of different tools, multiply the cutting stroke by the maximum strokes per minute. The resulting figure will be a truer measure of the tool's real cutting ability.

Orbital. One of the most recent innovations to saber saws is the orbital feature. In orbital action the

177

Saber Saw Basics

OFF TO THE RACES

This saber saw race shows how far you can cut in 15 seconds with one of three saber saws. The top tool is a professional-model tool with a 13/16 in. stroke moving at 3,200 strokes per minute. The middle tool is a consumer-grade model with a 5/8 in. stroke at 3,200 strokes per minute and is rated at 3.2 amps. The bottom tool is a consumer-grade saber saw with a 5/8 in. stroke at 3,200 strokes per minute and is rated at 3.0 amps.

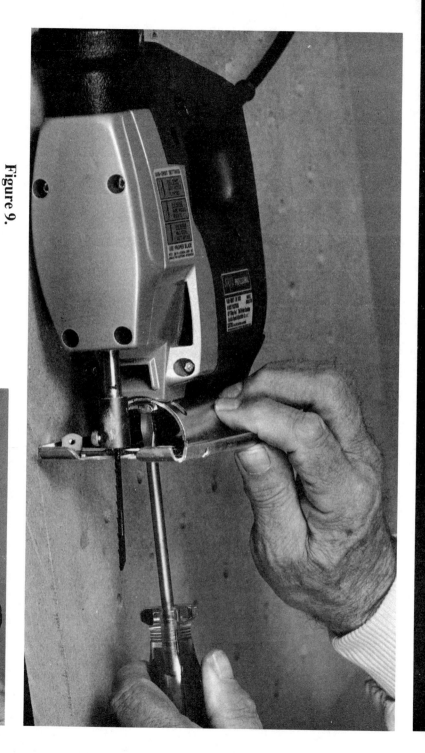

Figure 9.
To cut a miter, loosen the pad's holding screw and tilt the pad to the desired angle. Retighten the holding screw.

blade moves forward, into the wood when it cuts (up stroke) and away on the cleaning stroke (down stroke).

The orbital cut makes a faster but rougher cut. In professional models the tool can cut 2x4s as fast as a circular saw. For rough home framing, the orbital saber saw is a must.

This tool has an orbital and a normal setting. Some tools allow you to select from four orbital settings.

Power. Tool manufacturers no longer label tools in terms of horsepower, and instead measure tool power in amps. Like horsepower, as you increase the amperage, the more powerful the tool becomes. Most of us, however, have difficulty relating to amperage ratings.

179

Figure 10.
Here we are using a shop-made T-square to guide the saber saw while cutting a 45 degree bevel.

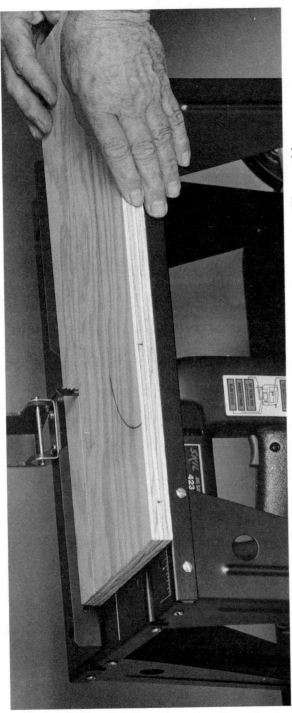

Figure 11.

A jigsaw table equipped with a wide, coarse-cutting blade does a good job of ripping lumber. The blade guard is lifted for clarity.

The good news is that you can go to a home center and check out the amperage ratings among tool manufacturers and models. This will familiarize you with the more common amperage settings and with the effect amperage has on the tool's price.

Professional vs. Consumer. There is a world of difference between the professional and consumer grades of saber saws — the professional models win, hands down!

You really won't appreciate the difference until you compare cutting with a consumer grade tool and cutting with a professional model. Professional tools are heavier, feel better and cut faster.

With a professional tool you will feel and see the result of power — a shorter stroke and a more vibration-free tool. If you buy a professional tool, you will undoubtedly depend on it much more.

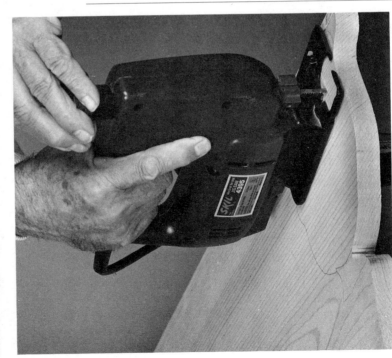

Figure 12.

This saber saw has scrolling ability. Unlock the scroll lock and turn the handle to the desired angle. Make your cuts.

How-to photographs are courtesy of Skil Corporation.

Figure 13.

Here is a close-up of a cut using a plywood cutting blade on the saber saw. Compare the edges and splintering with the photo below.

Figure 14.

A saber saw blade with eight teeth per inch was used in concert with orbital action to yield a rough cut. Compare the edges and splintering with the photo above.

BLADES. Most saber saw users know that blades come in a variety of teeth per inch, widths and lengths. Most do not know when to change the blade, however.

If you are using last year's blade, it is time to change. You can stretch the mileage out of the saber saw blade, but the cutting will be slow and the cuts probably will not be square. Use new, sharp blades for faster, smoother cutting.

Most saber saw blades are universal, which means they fit on almost any make of saber saw. Some professional blades cut on both the up and down stroke.

TECHNIQUES. Our photography shows you a number of techniques for using saber saws.

We show you the basics, but there is a lot more to be said about saber saws. For further information, check your local library.

❖

Saber Saw Patterns

e are very pleased to offer you this selection of patterns that can be cut with a saber saw. Our project opener, the book rack, is a simple project for beginning woodworkers. Our goal in providing you with this section is to present to you both simple and unique saber saw patterns.

We have selected the book rack because many of the other patterns can be adapted to replace the rectangular shape of the bookends.

BOOK RACK. This sliding book rack is an ideal accessory for the kitchen, bedroom or den.

Cut each of the three rectangular workpieces to size with a saber saw. Use a wide plywood cutting blade, cutting right up to the edge of the cutting line.

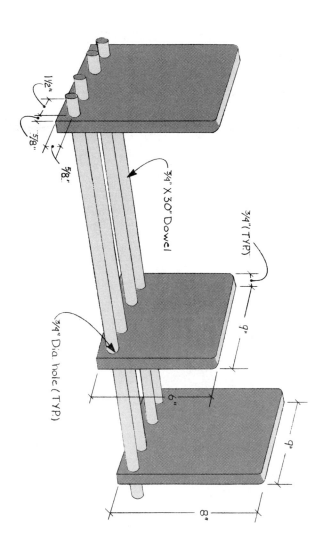

1/2"

5/8"

5/8"

3/4" X 30" Dowel

3/4" (TYP.)

9"

3/4" Dia. hole (TYP.)

6"

9"

8"

This project is courtesy of Georgia-Pacific Corporation, 133 Peachtree St. N.E., P.O. Box 105605, Atlanta, GA 30348.

Saber Saw Patterns

Then drill four ¾ in. diameter holes into each of these workpieces. Make sure that all of the holes are perpendicular and exact.

The ideal method for drilling these holes is to use a ¾ in. Forstner bit installed in your drill press. Drill all three workpieces at one time, making sure that the workpieces are clamped securely. Also, use a backup board to prevent the wood from splintering.

Now, use your saber saw to cut each of the four ¾ in. diameter dowels to the proper length.

Finish sand the entire project. Then mix about 2 oz. of bleached beeswax or white paraffin with an equal amount of turpentine in a jar. Allow it to stand overnight or until it turns into a paste. Spread this mixture over the surfaces of the workpieces, including the dowels. Use the wax sparingly, and buff it to a warm gloss.

Insert the dowels through each of the rectangular workpieces. Then glue the end workpieces. Then glue the end workpieces, allowing 1 in. of each of the dowels to extend beyond the outside of the end workpieces.

Predrill ¹⁄₁₆ in. holes from underneath the two end pieces and drive a small finishing nail into each dowel.

OTHER PATTERNS. The following patterns are compliments of the Skil booklet entitled **Getting the Most from your Skil Scrolling Jig Saw** by Hugh Foster. Some patterns are full size and can be traced onto a workpiece with the aid of graphite paper. Others will need to be enlarged, using a pantograph or a copy machine.

It doesn't matter what material you use when cutting the patterns; however, you will find that ½ in. or ¾ in. exterior-grade plywood will work best for outdoor projects. If you are going to place the projects in your garden or backyard, attach a 1x2 post to the project for stability. Also, use exterior stains and paints to give each project a unique look.

We hope you enjoy this section, and we look forward to seeing some of your project photos.

❖

Show off your woodworking skills with this selection of saber saw patterns.

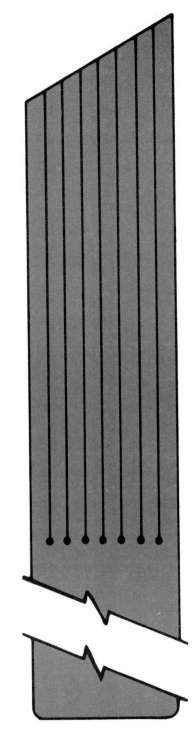

FEATHER BOARD

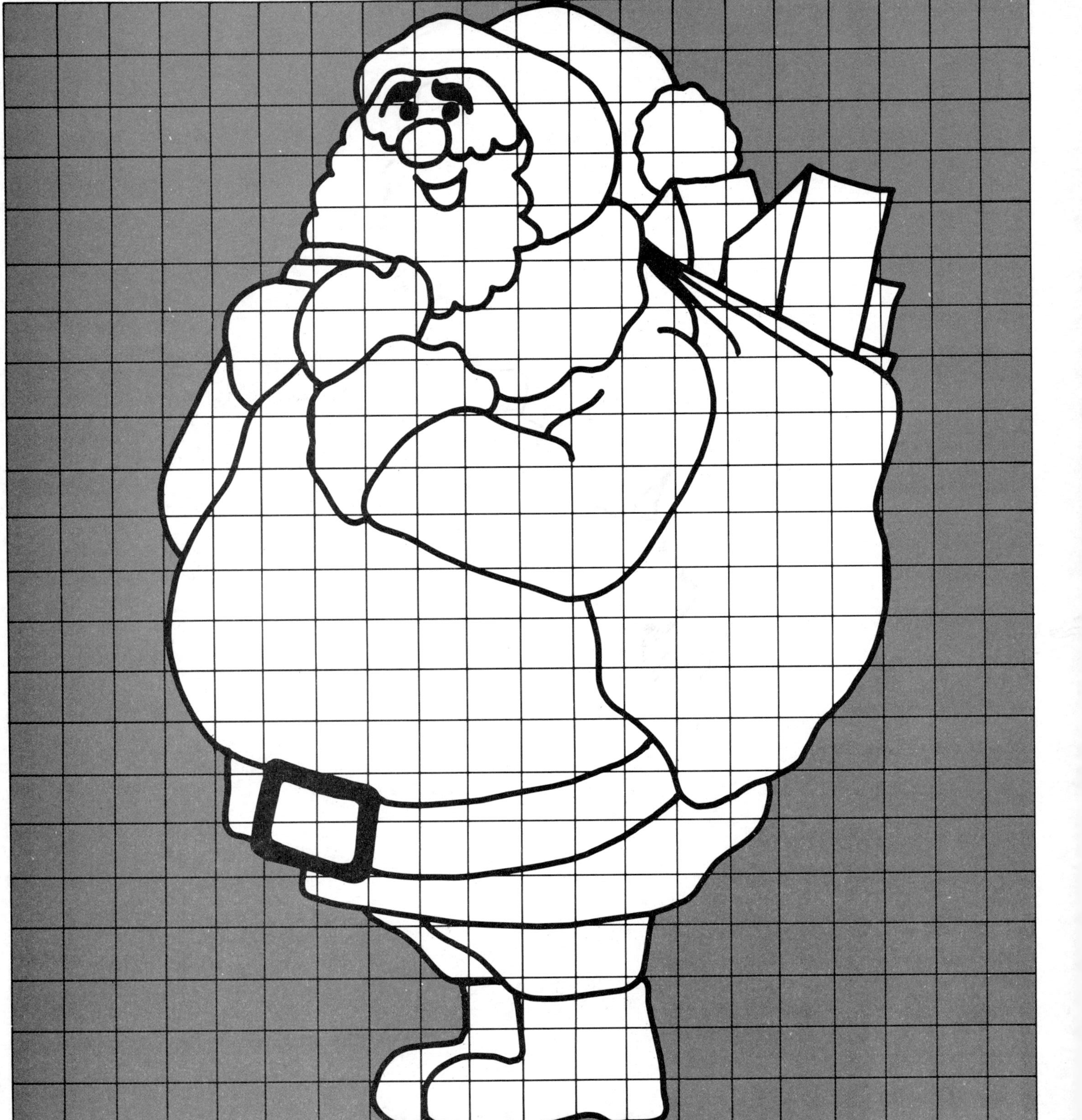

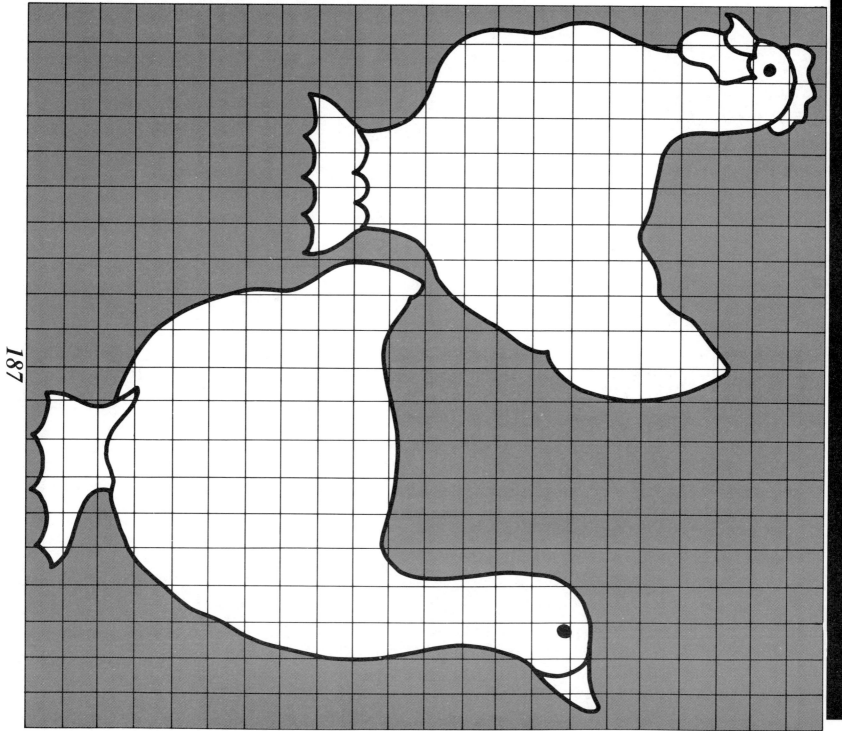

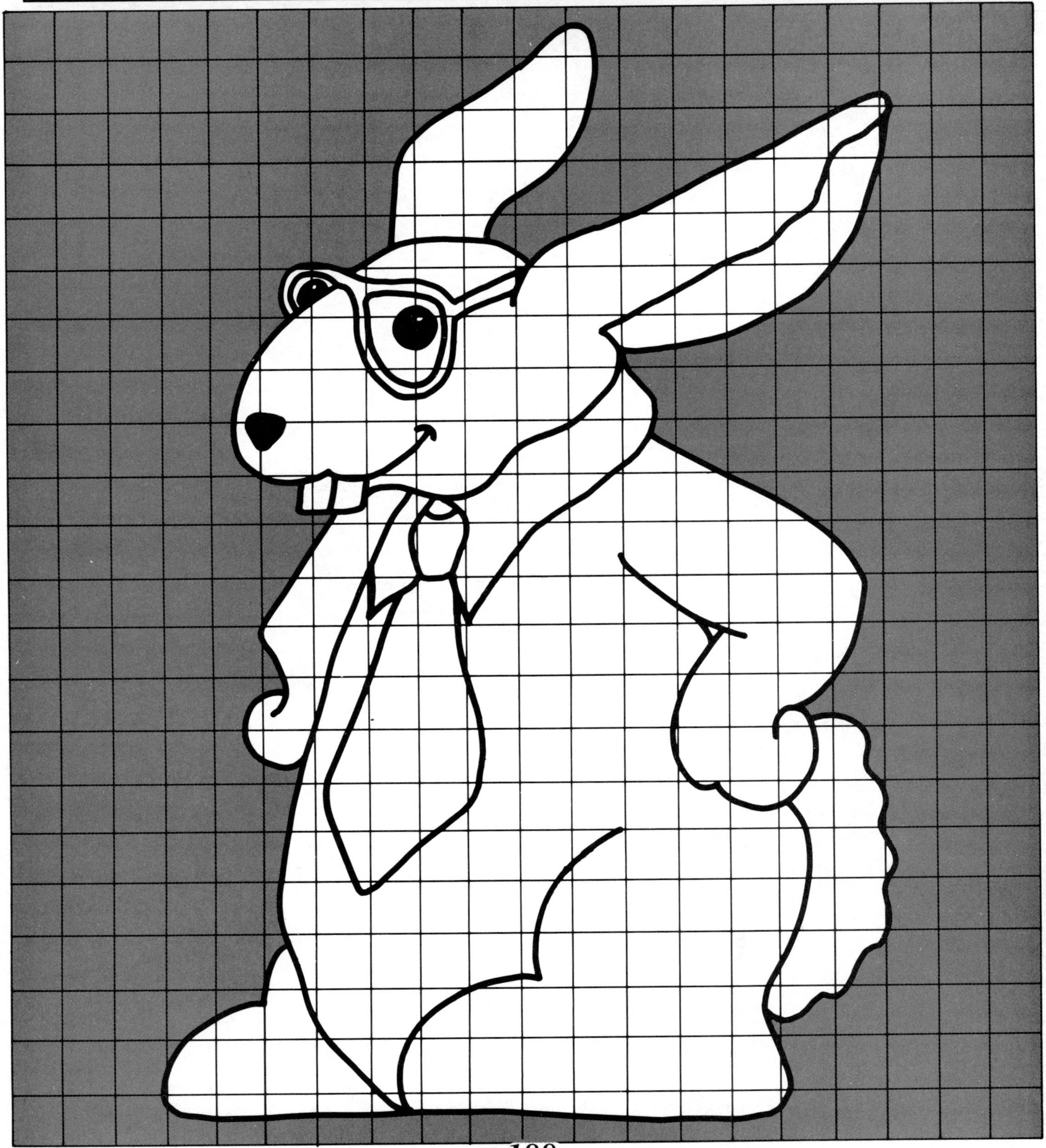

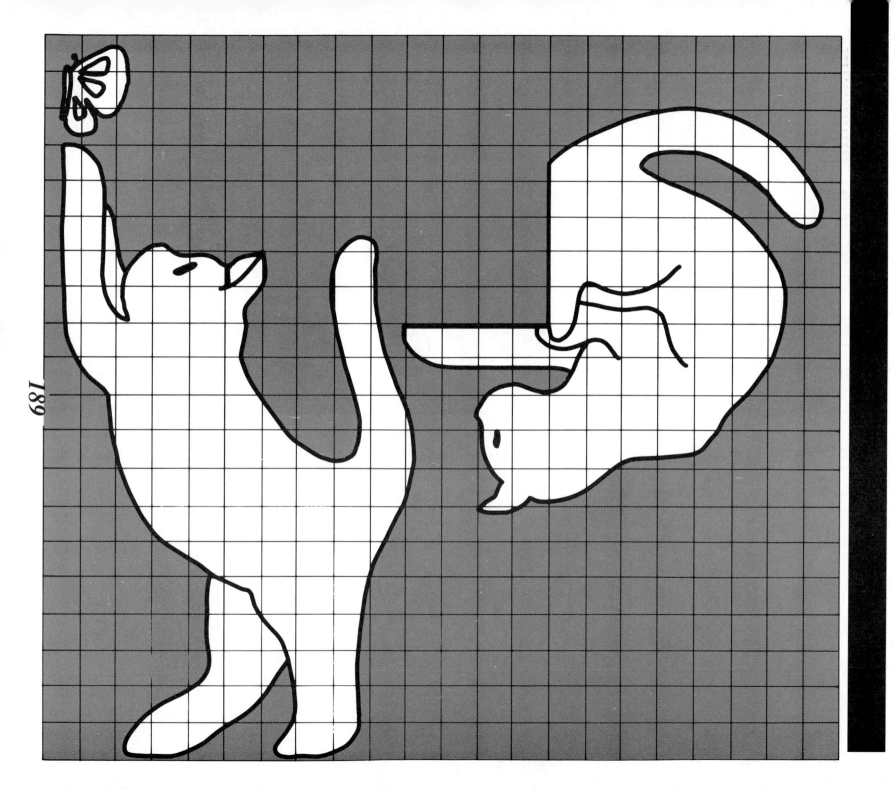

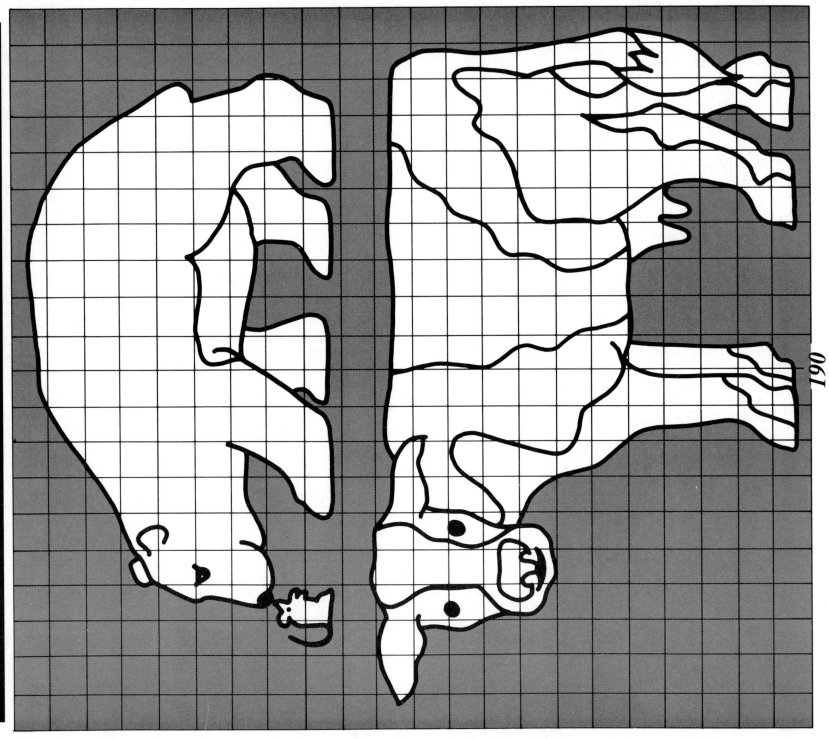

INDEX

SOURCES

PLAN AND PROJECT SUPPLIERS

American Plywood Association
P.O. Box 11700
Tacoma, WA 98411
(206) 565-6600

California Redwood Association
405 Enfrente Dr., Suite 200
Novato, CA 94949
(415) 382-0662

Georgia-Pacific Corporation
133 Peachtree St. N.E.
P.O. Box 105605
Atlanta, GA 30348
(404) 521-4741

TOOL SUPPLIERS

Dremel*
4915 21st St.
Racine, WI 53406
(414) 554-1390

Sears Catalog
7447 Skokie Blvd.
Skokie, IL 60077

Skil Corporation*
4300 West Peterson Ave.
Chicago, IL 60646
(312) 286-7330

Vermont American Tool Company*
P.O. Box 340
Lincolnton, NC 28093
(704) 735-7464

* Special thanks to Skil, Dremel and Vermont American for their cosponsorship of this book.